Panic-Proof Investing

Panic-Proof

Investing:

Lessons in Profitable Investing from a Market Wizard

THOMAS F. BASSO

JOHN WILEY & SONS, INC.
New York · Chichester · Brisbane · Toronto · Singapore

Copyright 1994 by Trendstat Capital Management
Published by John Wiley & Sons, Inc.

Library of Congress Cataloging-in-Publication Data:

Basso, Thomas F.
    Panic-proof investing: lessons in profitable investing from a market
    wizard/Thomas F. Basso
        p.   cm.
    ISBN 0-471-03024-4

Printed in the United States of America

10   9   8   7   6   5   4   3   2   1

Acknowledgments

So many have helped me with this project. I would like to thank my wife, Sue, for putting up with our somewhat unusual lifestyle revolving around the world's financial markets. Her advice and dedication have helped make our business a success.

Thanks also to George, Jean, Lou, Donna, Dave, and Kathy, our group of dedicated professionals at Trendstat. I'd have a hard time managing anyone's money without them.

I very much appreciate the comments and suggestions I received from Sandy and Betsy Venitt in Phoenix. Their friendship, encouragement, and ability to translate financial lingo into understandable English was invaluable.

Thanks to Carl Bolz, a friend and fellow golfer, the book has a lot fewer problems with grammar and spelling. His editing was superb.

I would also give my regards to John Holm, who created illustrations that capture exactly the points I was trying to make and helped give the book the friendly feel I wanted.

Finally, thanks to Dr. Van K. Tharp and Adrienne Toghraie, who long ago invited me to a seminar on investment psychology. At that seminar, I realized the need for my clients to know more about this topic. About one year later, at another of their seminars, I thought of writing this book. They have helped me understand more about how the human mind works, and how I have been able to succeed in trading and the investment management business, where others have struggled.

Preface

In the world of speculative trading, approximately one-third of all existing traders are forced to stop trading each year. This means that a third of them either lose most of their money or, at least, become sufficiently discouraged to stop trading. Furthermore, the statistics seem to indicate that about 90 to 95 percent of all speculative traders lose money each year, while only a fraction of a percentage of traders make really big money. When you think about it, this makes sense. It takes a lot of small losers to total the amount gained by the largest traders. More important, the super traders tend to have certain psychological characteristics that the average person fails to nurture and develop.

The situation is not much better when it comes to turning one's money over to a financial advisor. Why? First, most advisors fail to outperform the market averages. Second, the same psychological factors that cause the average person to lose result in the average person making mistakes in dealing with money managers. For example, the average trader will invest with the hot money manager right before the big drawdown, and then withdraw his money right before the next upturn in his performance.

So what separates the top traders from the average person? Many of the best traders in the world have attained that status because they realize the importance of their own psychology to their success. For example, one trader, who is profiled in Jack Schwager's book, *Market Wizards,* said that he started out by managing about a dozen small accounts in the late 1960s. Over the years, he noticed that some of the accounts made a lot of money while other accounts did not. Yet he was trading all of his managed accounts the same way. The only variable was when the clients added or withdrew money. Generally, those who made the most money kept their money with him. Those who made the least money tended to pull their money out after a losing streak, usually just prior to the onset of some big profits, and would add money after a long winning streak, just prior to a drawdown in the account. This trader also said that he noticed parallels in the personal lives of these people. Those who tended to make money had very successful lives. Those who lost money tended to lose in whatever enterprise they undertook. Do you think this was a coincidence, perhaps? I think not! This trader eventually gave up managing other people's money, partly because he cared to deal only with his own emotional ups and downs, not those of his clients.

Another great trader, portrayed in Jack Schwager's latest book entitled *The New Market Wizards,* took a different path in terms of managing money. He has elected to actively deal with the problems of the small investor. That trader is the author of this book, Tom Basso. Tom was originally a founder of an investment advisory firm called Kennedy Capital Management. He and his partners broke up over some disagreements in the firm's direction. Tom's former partner took over the management of all of the large company accounts, while Tom's investment firm retained the management of the individual investor accounts. Since that time, Tom has consistently performed well while helping the individual investor.

As a result, I cannot imagine anyone more qualified than Tom Basso to write a book directed toward surviving as a client of a financial advisor. Tom really wants to work with and help the small investor. In an interview that I did with Tom several years ago, he made the following statement:

"A lot of the things I started creating at that point in 1984 involved solving some of my own investing problems and knowing that there must be thousands of other people out there with the same problems. Life became a lot more fun at that point. I controlled my own destiny a lot more. I had more input into the strategic direction we were going. I knew where I wanted to go. I wanted to approach the markets from an econometric viewpoint; to improve my ability to control risk; to continue to help people; and to get myself in a position where I could spend the time helping other people with investments."

Tom has another equally important qualification for writing this book in that, in my opinion, he is a model trader. Let me illustrate why I believe that.

In January 1989 I gave a talk at the Managed Accounts Reports (MAR) Conference on the Psychology of Successful Money Management. Part of that talk included a discussion of self-esteem and how it affects trading performance. In short, I told the group that people tend to create their universe according to their beliefs, and that one of the most significant levels of belief was their belief about themselves—their self-esteem. In fact, beliefs tend to form a hierarchy, with beliefs about oneself being among the most significant. Furthermore, people who feel good about themselves are more likely to be successful investors and traders. Most people don't feel that good about themselves, unfortunately, which is a major reason for the poor market performance demonstrated by the general public.

Let me give you a specific example of how low self-esteem impairs trading performance by talking about Bill, a client of mine whose name I've changed to protect his identity. Bill, due to various events that occurred early in his childhood, did not really like himself or feel worthy of success. He kept believing that if he could be successful in the markets, he would then like himself. What happened, however, was that he continued to do things to sabotage his trading performance and justify the way he felt about himself. Why? It was because whatever Bill believed about himself was right, and he performed according to those beliefs. What Bill needed to do was to improve his self-image and, as a result of that improvement, good performance would tend to follow. Furthermore, once Bill had changed his self-image, his trading performance improved dramatically.

At the 1989 MAR Conference I presented the over 400 attendees with a questionnaire designed to measure self-esteem. The scores on the test can range from zero to 40, with zero indicating the highest level of self esteem. When I asked the audience how many people had scored five or less on the test, only one person raised a hand. That person was Tom Basso. I had a chance to talk with Tom in person later that day, and came to the conclusion that Tom had one of the highest levels of self-esteem of anyone I had ever met. Tom and I have subsequently become good friends, and I can now say that my impression of Tom has endured the test of time.

In Tom's own words:

"I think it's important for a trader to have high self-esteem—not letting his ego get in the way of the discipline that's required to be a good trader. Therefore, this allows the trader to concentrate on the process of trading and let the results fall where they may. More often than not, if you do a good job of trading, the results will be very good."

Jack Schwager, author of the book *Market Wizards: Interviews with Top Traders,* interviewed Tom after a Peak Performance Trading seminar that we did together in New York in 1991. His conclusion was that of all the traders he had interviewed, Tom was the person he would most like to model in his personal trading. Once again, I agree, and we continually invite Tom back to our seminars to answer questions as a model trader.

Another reason that I am so delighted to write a preface for Tom's book is that I know he understands the key elements for successful performance. Tom considers himself to be a businessman first and a trader second. His business approach to the markets is quite incredible. He is organized, and plans every possible event in his mind well before it could possibly happen. Why not do that? Detailed planning is probably one of the most crucial elements to trading success, and Tom does it as well as anyone I know. For example, Tom says:

"As life has gotten more complex with all the clients we have and the businesses we have gotten into, there's going to be a high probability that certain things will happen. There's going to be a certain percentage of client calls; a certain percent of trading problems; and a certain amount of computer malfunctions or computer programming problems. Usually, I'm thinking through them as I drive to work every morning—sort of scoping out the day."

Tom always makes himself available to people at our Peak Performance Trading seminars for giving advice and answering questions. Although we devote a specific portion of the seminar for Tom to answer questions, he makes himself available throughout the entire seminar, during the evenings, and even after the seminar is over. Moreover, Tom sets aside part of each afternoon for helping his clients with their personal concerns about how their money is being managed, and he is quite generous with his advice. I'm sure this book would have been impossible for Tom to write without his many years of experience giving advice to clients.

"I've tried as much as possible to consider that the money I'm managing is the client's money. It's not mine. Never, ever forget that. As one broker on the West Coast puts it, 'In the money management industry we sell bottom line and peace of mind.' I have maintained over the years that peace of mind is more important than the bottom line. If the client doesn't have peace of mind, he leaves. And peace of mind doesn't necessarily have anything to do with the bottom line. If you can match the client's desires with what you're trying to do for him, then you're going to have a happy client for many years to come."

Tom is an incredible person, and I am delighted that he is willing to share some of his insights in a simple, down-to-earth format that every investor can understand.

Van K. Tharp, Ph.D.
Van K. Tharp and Associates, Inc.

Contents ━━━━━━━━━━━━━━

Introduction ━━━━━━━━━━━━━

I have had many rewarding experiences in my career as a money manager. One of them has to be writing this book. I've been managing money for others for around 17 years, but I remain amazed at how poorly clients manage their financial affairs. I have met countless people who have spent their lives struggling with investments. Many are bitter at the money management community, some with good cause. Others simply lack the knowledge of how to sensibly approach the question of investing assets.

Unfortunately, all the stories in this book are true. In some cases, I've taken two real situations and combined them to make more points, but they remain real situations. Some are sad. Some are humorous. All are educational.

This book was originally conceived as required reading for my money management clients. My theory was that the smarter I make my clients, the more they will let me do for them. This should allow my firm to be more successful, since its success is tied to our clients' well-being. But later, at the encouragement of others, I thought I should make this book available to brokers/financial planners, money managers, and investors who could be helped by its contents.

I don't mean to offend any particular segment of the money management industry or any particular type of investment. There are good and bad stock portfolio managers, partnerships, futures trading programs, and brokers. I've pointed out some blemishes in the investment industry, but I want to emphasize that you can find honest, efficient investments and advisors in every area of investing. The bottom line is that we in the money management community have to look out for the clients and help make them more knowledgeable. The more the clients know about the process of successful investing, the more we can drive the bad guys out of the marketplace and the fewer laws society will require to protect investors.

I dedicate this book to all those investors who want to take the first step on the road to less frustration in managing their money.

I hope you enjoy the book.

Tom Basso

Panic-Proof Investing

Chapter One ━━━━━━

The Frustrated
Investor

Have you ever blamed your broker, insurance agent, advisor, or financial planner for that lousy partnership he sold you? How about your feelings toward those assorted life insurance policies that you didn't understand? Maybe you're not very happy with your good friend who confidentially gave you a hot tip on a great stock that, promptly after your purchase, hit the skids and hasn't since seen the light of day. That investment advisor with the hot track record and no losing years is now suffering his first down year—right after you gave him your money to manage. It seems everywhere you turn you hear about investors getting hurt by investment scams, bad deals, or, at a minimum, poor decisions and timing. You start thinking that no investor is immune to the shifting winds of investment fortune.

But what about that guy you knew at work who seemed uncanny at picking market tops and bottoms? Or that retired businesswoman at church who has done so well with her investments? Now that you think about it, there's a magazine article now and then about some investor who over the years has produced some dazzling success stories in the investment world. You start thinking, "This could be me," and then invest in something, only to have the markets remind you that investing success is apparently meant for someone else. If this sounds familiar, you may be a frustrated investor. Perhaps you've never invested at all, and are trying to avoid becoming a frustrated investor. No matter what your situation, this book should be useful for you since it deals with the common link to these potential frustrations: *your own mind and how you use it*. My years as a registered money manager have provided me with so many vivid examples of how investors can shoot themselves in the foot, I had a difficult time condensing it down to this brief collection of stories and thoughts.

Let us now embark on a journey to the center of our minds, where all things start and all things are possible.

Chapter Two ——————

—————— ## Three Areas
of Investing Success

Investors are always searching for the Holy Grail investment that will answer all their concerns about making money. Most people have adopted what I call the Universal Investment Objective: "Make me as much money as you can with as little risk as possible." Let's consider the story of Al Marshall.

Al was a student of the markets, and worked with various stockbrokers. He enjoyed the challenge of investing. Although he was not very successful, Al never gave up hope of improving his performance. He purchased a few investing systems, followed several different newsletters on investing, and hired two money managers to handle part of his portfolio.

After many years, the challenge of investing started to get a little frustrating. It seemed that every new strategy that Al used would work for a while, but then, just as he got his hopes up, they would be dashed along with the value of his investments. He would then search out a better way, and try that approach, only to have the same thing happen again. Al kept thinking, "When will my hard work pay off?" What can be learned from this brief example?

Requirements for Success

I have observed many successful investors, and they all seem to have three things in place. First, *they have a strategy* of some sort that gets them into and out of an investment. Second, *they have risk or money management concepts* that preserve their assets when the investments don't work out the way they thought they would. Third, and most important, *they have a good understanding of themselves, and they have structured their investments to suit their situation, resources, and personality.*

Investment Strategy

Investment strategy is what most investors worry about. They think, "If I can just find the right broker or trading system, I can finally be a successful investor." They go from one idea to the next, frustrated by their lack of success.

Successful investors do need a strategy, but it doesn't have to be difficult to develop. Some of the old clichés give you a hint of some of the appropriate characteristics of a successful strategy. "Buy low, sell high," and, "Cut your losses short, let your gains run," are useful to a degree. *Most important, however, your investments should fit your situation, resources, and skill level.* For example, if following one strategy requires daily contact with the market and you travel a lot, then look for longer-term strategy that doesn't require as much day-to-day attention. Remember, in searching for or developing an investment strategy, simple things work the best. The easier the system or strategy, the more likely you will understand it, be comfortable with it, and, therefore, use it.

Don't spend all your time searching for the perfect strategy. It doesn't exist. Every strategy will have to face tough market periods when it appears to not be working. It was foolish for Al to run to a new investment every time his current one faced challenging market conditions. Simply develop something that seems logical for your situation and fits you. *The area of searching for and developing a trading strategy of where to buy and where to sell is the* least important *area of investing success.*

Money Management

The second and more important area is that of money management. I have seen countless investing strategies hurt investors because of the use of excessive leverage or a lack of diversification. Real estate, by itself, is not bad. But most of the no-money-down, instant real estate tycoons are licking their wounds and searching for cash or ways out of their leveraged nightmare. This effect of leverage can be found in many other investments. You can buy bonds, stocks, and mutual funds on margin. You can buy very small penny stocks that are very leveraged vehicles. Futures and options can be used as very leveraged investments, if the investor chooses to use them in that fashion.

You have to be able to come back tomorrow and play the game again. If you risk too much or put too much leverage into an investment, you can wipe yourself out and be out of the game. A successful, balanced investor does not take wild, long shots in an attempt to make a killing. *He assesses the calculated risk and invests an amount appropriate for taking on the potential risk and the potential reward. He understands that every investment has risk and reward and that he can take positive steps to affect the outcome of his investment using sensible money management techniques.* These money management techniques should include proper diversification by market, by manager, and by technique. They should also include good market selection and investing only a small percentage of the total portfolio in any one position.

Understanding Yourself

The *final, and* most important, *area of investing success is understanding how you will react to various investment scenarios.* Al constantly moved on to other investments. He did that because he was not comfortable with each investment he selected. One of the major reasons why investors are uncomfortable with their investment is they haven't matched themselves to the investment. If you are a hands-on person and want to get involved in the day-to-day decision making, then don't hire a money manager to manage your assets. You'll just end up frustrated, because day-to-day decisions will be made without your input. If, on the other hand, you are a person who looks at the big picture and doesn't want to worry about details, be careful working with a broker who calls you often with ideas to buy or sell. You'll have a tendency to just say, "Whatever you think is best," and you may not follow your long-term strategies.

If you have an "I don't know much about investing" attitude, you might want to hire someone with financial expertise to help you.

However, the potential pitfalls are many and most of the time you will still face some of the same frustrations that you would have had if you yourself had invested. Perhaps the thing to do would be to change to an "I don't know much about investing, but I'm going to learn more about it" attitude.

Comfort has a lot to do with being a successful, balanced investor. When an investment is appropriate for an investor, it becomes almost as easy as breathing. A balanced investor understands the overall strategy, does a good job of diversifying and managing the risks, and feels comfortable that the investment suits his or her personality. Before jumping into an investment strategy, think about what type of person you are. Are you impulsive, decisive, strategic, or tactical? Do you like to be involved or remain distant from the day-to-day decisions?

Ask yourself what is required of you and others to achieve the expected rates of return. Design your investment program around yourself. If you feel unable to do so due to lack of knowledge about investments, consult a financial advisor with whom you feel comfortable and tell him or her that you want to design a program that fits you. What you don't need is to be sold the latest, greatest fad investment idea that everyone is buying. *The more comfortable your investments feel to you, the easier it will be to be a successful, balanced investor.*

Chapter Three

Your Perceptions
Are Different from Others'

Each investor comes to the investing arena with a different set of experiences, amount of knowledge, and set of beliefs about the way the world works. We are all individuals. No two investors are exactly the same. Because we are all different, we perceive the world around us with our own biases and beliefs. Perhaps an example will clarify this concept.

Hugh Martin grew up in a working-class environment. His parents worked hard to make ends meet. Luxuries were hard to come by due to lack of money. The Martins were comfortable, but not wealthy. Hugh's parents frequently told him that money was evil, and that wealthy people had all sorts of problems and were very unhappy.

As Hugh grew up, he wished for a better life. His friends always seemed to buy things he couldn't afford. He noticed that his friends frequently didn't have a lot of money either, but spent as if they did. They would get themselves into positions where they would have to borrow on their credit cards, take a home equity loan, or hit up a friend for some spending cash. Hugh felt that spending beyond their means was a foolish way for them to manage their finances.

But Hugh Martin still had a desire to be truly wealthy so he could have the luxuries while still living within his means. He maintained a frugal lifestyle and saved some money to invest.

Hugh was careful when he started looking into investments. He concentrated on the costs of various investment alternatives. He analyzed stocks, and bought them cheap. He negotiated with bond traders on the price he'd pay for certain bond issues. He patiently waited for real estate deals that made sense. To many, Hugh appeared to be on the path to investment success.

But the more Hugh experienced success, the more uncomfortable he was with his position in life. He remembered his parents telling him that money is evil, and he remembered that he should live within his means. He wondered what his friends thought of him now that he had acquired some wealth. Would they think he was evil? Would they believe that he had obtained his money by illegal or immoral means?

He found it much easier to avoid his friends and live the life of a recluse. If he didn't spend money on personal luxuries, maybe it wouldn't be as apparent that he had a lot of it. Maybe, too, people would like him more. He decided that holding on to his investment successes made more sense than making profits. If he didn't sell his investments, they were not really his to spend on unnecessary luxuries. He watched investment after investment become overvalued and move down, but refused to make a move to protect the profits. Most of his investments became mediocre, long-term positions. As the years went by, he became a frustrated investor, wondering why he wasn't more successful and happy with the results of his hard work.

Hugh Martin started out with some successes in his investments. He was driven to be better off financially. His friends thought he was successful, but he was not happy or balanced. Let's analyze some of the important points of Hugh's story.

Money Is Not Evil

Money is simply money. It is nothing more, nothing less. It is simply a way for people to transfer goods and services to each other without bartering. Some wealthy people are happy; others are miserable.

There are also happy and unhappy individuals with less wealth. Most people ultimately want to be happy or content. They think, "I'll be happy when I retire," or "If I have a lot of money I'll be able to buy a better life for myself and my family and be more content with my life." *Happiness or contentment in life will not come and go with an increase or decrease in a checking account balance.*

A few years ago, a successful client of mine sold, for a sizable sum of money, a microwave network he had built from nothing. I was a little more naive in those days, and commented that, "I guess you've got it made now." He looked at me and said, "Son your first million dollars will buy you all the necessities of daily life. You can afford a nice car, nice house, put food on the table and clothes on your back. The money I made on this deal will just go back into more invest-ments. My net worth is just the score of the game I'm playing." He was a very happy, content person. Part of the reason he was so balanced was his ability not to tie his ego or self-worth to his net worth. It was simply the score of the game.

When the famous futures trader, Richard Dennis, selected his apprentices, known as the "Turtles," he looked for game-playing experience. He obviously felt that the ability to play mental games like chess or cards improved a person's ability to deal with the mental challenges of investing. Some people refer to investing as a brain tease, a challenge, or an intellectual pursuit. Most successful investors realize that they'll never be perfect investors, but they can enjoy the process and challenge of getting better at it. They realize that improving their skills puts them on the road toward being perfect investors. At the same time, they are comfortable with the knowledge that they will never arrive at perfection. They simply enjoy the trip, and don't get obsessed with the final destination. *Separate your self-worth from your net worth if you want to be more successful at investing.*

The Same Event through Different Eyes

To many people, Hugh Martin was successful. However, Hugh didn't feel successful. Actually, he was miserable and uncomfortable about his financial success. The same event is often perceived by two different people two different ways. This happens around us every day of our lives. Sometimes kids say the most interesting things as they observe something from their viewpoint. Eyewitnesses may have slightly different versions of the same accident. Politicians have different visions of the current political situation. The traveling sales representative hates getting on a plane, while the homemaker longs for an out-of-town trip. One employee considers her job boring, while another in the same position seems excited and enjoys the challenge.

The lesson to be learned here is that *your universe exists according to your own set of beliefs. Everything you perceive is structured by your belief system.* Successful investors understand that other investors may have a different set of beliefs that, to those other investors, are just as important and real. Think about how comedians make us laugh by taking routine things that we experience every day and getting us to see them from a different viewpoint. Normal, mundane, unexciting events suddenly become hilarious. *Keep your mind flexible and open to new ideas.*

Most frustrated investors have beliefs that do not support successful investing. They may believe they shouldn't take responsibility or that wealthy people are unhappy. They might believe that floor traders are always manipulating the market against them or that investing is a form of entertainment. If your beliefs do not support investing success, you will constantly struggle and have a difficult time achieving the success you seek.

Examine some of your beliefs about investing, and analyze how useful they are to your improvement as an investor. For example, many would say that futures investments are risky. Yet it is how you manage a futures portfolio that makes it risky or conservative. It is inappropriate to place labels on various markets as conservative or risky. Without knowing how the investment is to be managed and how much leverage there is, how can anyone say that an investment is risky or conservative? What gives investors the idea that they can place labels on an investment without knowing anything about how it is to be managed? If the investor believes the risky label that a futures portfolio generally has, he doesn't examine a futures portfolio at all. On the other hand, he might believe that it could be either risky or conservative. That way, he is willing to examine more details about some of the advantages and disadvantages of a futures investment and may conclude it can fit in his overall portfolio. *If your beliefs are not useful, consider changing them or exploring other ways of looking at the situation.*

Chapter Four

Who's to Blame?

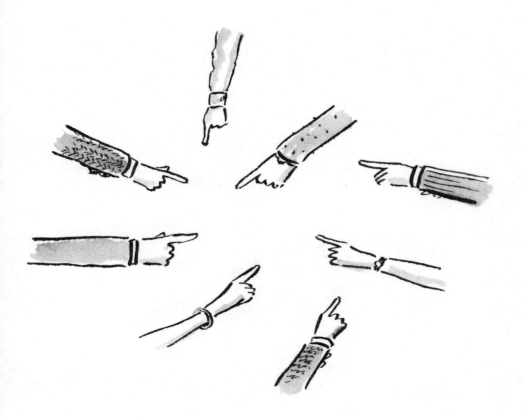

A healthy way of looking at investing, and life for that matter, is that you are responsible for what happens to you. I'm not trying to get into any debates here about spiritual beliefs. I am saying that if you trace a series of events back to their origins, *most events in your life are dramatically affected by a decision you made somewhere in time or the way you chose to respond to some external event.*

Mr. Smith was a small businessman who ran a successful auto parts store. One day he heard a rumor from one of his suppliers, Mr. Green. Mr. Green indicated that Large Auto Parts, Inc. (LAP), a major parts manufacturing company, was going to buy out Small Parts, Inc. (SPI), a minor company that competed with LAP. Mr. Green continued on about how LAP was loaded with cash and would be expanding its market share. Mr. Green also told Mr. Smith that he had just picked up some LAP shares, deciding that it just had to go up. For the next few days, Mr. Smith watched the newspaper for the quotations on LAP and any news of the acquisition. The price was moving up with the general market. Finally, he just had to have this stock. He checked with his brokerage firm for any research their analysts had on the company. The reply showed that LAP was loaded with cash and was financially stable. The broker was happy to purchase LAP for Mr. Smith. Based on Green's advice and an accommodating broker, Mr. Smith picked up a few hundred shares.

Within a few days, the news came out on the acquisition. LAP was trying to make a hostile takeover of SPI, a rival firm. The small company was not willing to be acquired, and wanted a higher price for its stock. The larger firm would increase the offer, but would have to reduce its stockpile of cash. Meanwhile, the general market started to slide. Mr. Smith's LAP stock was going down quickly. Reading the morning newspaper became a frustrating experience as Mr. Smith watched the stock sink lower and lower.

About a week later, Mr. Green stopped by the store. He informed Mr. Smith that when he heard that there were problems with the takeover, he had dumped his LAP stock and took a small loss. He was really glad he did, since the stock had gone much lower. Mr. Smith, who hadn't told Green that he had bought the stock, now became privately enraged at Mr. Green for talking about the company. In fact, why hadn't his broker stopped him from buying the stock? It must have been that commission the broker made. Mr. Smith decided to look for a new broker with a better research department.

Who's to blame here? Mr. Smith thinks that Mr. Green and the broker should share the blame. I think he should look a little closer to home. In this age of instant communication, information bombards the investor every day. The investor has to sort through this information to make decisions based on the facts he feels are relevant. Many wish it were the good old days when information flowed at a slower pace, but wishing for this will not reduce the information flow or help you keep pace with a fast-changing world.

Balancing the Mental Scenarios

There were a few points at which Mr. Smith could have changed the outcome. First, *he should have taken a more balanced look at the story he heard* from Mr. Green. It would not be difficult to balance the positive side of the story with a disclaimer, such as, "On the other hand, the deal might not go through as planned, or the general market might get weak." That alone might have been enough to cool Mr. Smith's excitement.

Most brokers and financial planners would agree that investments are sold, not bought. I don't believe that this is a big problem, since without the sales effort, most investors would never hear about new financial products that might be perfect for them. However, when an investment is sold to you, remember that generally the person doing the selling will have a tendency to tell you the 10 reasons this is a great deal. You may not get a complete list of all the reasons you should not make this investment. You must balance the scenarios yourself by asking questions, reading the literature, dreaming up adverse conditions for the investment, or questioning some of the selling points. The goal is to balance your mind between the reward and risk associated with the investment.

Mental Balancing of the Information Flow

Another decision point that Mr. Smith had was in his conversation with the broker. Brokers make their money when investors buy or sell. They are human beings, and their research departments don't have a lock on all the information in the world. When Mr. Smith heard the expected reply about the company he was interested in, he could have asked, "Why, and how much, will this potential acquisition affect the price of the stock? What is the likelihood of this acquisition actually happening?" He might have concluded at that point that the acquisition would have little effect on LAP, or that SPI would put up a battle. He could have given himself a more balanced state of mind.

I try to dream up alternative scenarios that the investment will face. What could go wrong with the investment? What type of tax law changes might affect the investment? What if there is a change in the management of the company in charge of the investment? What if the economy goes into another depression? Be innovative with your questions. If you are only getting a bunch of positive reasons to purchase the investment, then look for more negatives. If you are just finding negatives, then look for some reasons that favor the investment.

Create a Plan before Investing

The final decision point that I want to discuss is Mr. Smith's failure to minimize his losses. Mr. Green, when hearing of the problems with the acquisition, got out with a small loss. He put the loss behind him, and then positioned his mind in a positive state, looking for the next potentially good opportunity. Mr. Smith bought the stock based on Green's story and the advice of an accommodating broker. He gave himself no way to get out of the investment. Perhaps he thought Mr. Green would stop by and tell him when he should sell out. Maybe his broker would call and tell him. In reality, they are responsible for their actions, and Mr. Smith should be responsible for his.

The investor should ask himself several questions: "At what point will I get out of this investment if it goes the way I think it will go?

How will I get out of it if it doesn't go the way I think it will go? What ongoing information do I need to monitor this investment?" This sets up a plan that can be followed. *The investor must take the responsibility of setting up a plan for himself.* Even if he hires an advisor, he should decide under what circumstances he will continue with the advisor and under what circumstances he will fire the advisor. Mr. Green could have set up a plan to buy the stock with a stop loss in place to protect the investment. If the stock went up, he could have let it run. If the stock went down, he could have sold out immediately, protecting his assets. Both outcomes could have been done without a lot of thought or time on Mr. Green's part. By not having a plan, he opened himself up to severe loss.

You can take advantage of this advice by setting up a plan for how you will exit an investment before making the purchase. In so doing, you will take some of the emotion out of executing the plan and reduce your potential frustration over knowing when to sell it.

In another example, Mrs. Perkins, age 63 and a widow of five years, found herself in a bit of a fix. Her late husband, Harry, had always managed the family finances. He had put together a portfolio of quality stocks and bonds that would provide a steady income flow for retirement. His untimely death left Mrs. Perkins with a very comfortable financial picture. But Mr. Perkins' broker, Mike Stone of Investments Unlimited, Inc., retired shortly after Mr. Perkins' passing, leaving Mrs. Perkins with no financial advisor. Her brokerage firm was quick to replace Mr. Stone with Tom Grant, since it didn't want to lose such a stable, profitable client. The new broker was a self-proclaimed expert in financial/estate planning, and felt strongly that Mrs. Perkins should pay more attention to reducing income and estate taxes. He presented her with a complicated, detailed plan. Part of the money would be reinvested in some high-yield real estate partnerships sponsored by his firm; the rest would be reinvested in safe insurance products from major insurance companies to provide tax-deferred benefits.

This sounded good to Mrs. Perkins, since she thought that her spouse would have encouraged her to better herself. Although this new financial advisor was a little young, he seemed to know his business.

Besides, her brokerage firm had recommended him. She decided to go on with the rest of her life and proceed with the new plan. She felt relieved to have made the decision, and felt her new advisor would help her with future investment advice.

The checks came in regularly for the first two years. Then a notice came from one of the partnerships stating they were suspending the income payments. They were going to reorganize, and hoped the situation would improve. When asked about it, her broker brushed it off as a minor problem, saying he would look into the details. Having someone to rely on who knew what he was doing comforted Mrs. Perkins, because this was foreign to her.

Another year went by, and then the news came out that the state was taking over the insurance company that held one of Mrs. Perkins' annuities. Heavy losses in junk bonds and the lack of surplus prompted the move. Temporarily, her annuity was to be frozen, and she would no longer receive any income from the investment. The state would audit the company's books and figure out what was going on, which could take many months, perhaps years. Mrs. Perkins started to worry, since this was a large portion of her income. With the partnership's suspended payments, she was going to be a little short on money. The broker indicated that she should be patient. Since the state was taking over, her assets were now protected, and, after some auditing, the company would probably be absorbed by a higher-quality insurance company. Mrs. Perkins, although not completely comfortable about the situation, agreed to grit her teeth and be patient.

Unfortunately, things continued to deteriorate to the point where Mrs. Perkins' income was not enough to meet her living expenses. Another of her big holdings, a partnership investment, ceased making income payments. It was about then that her broker, Tom Grant, got a new position wholesaling for a large, very successful, Boston-based mutual fund group. The prospect of dealing with yet another broker become too much to bear. Mrs. Perkins didn't know what to do. She considered declaring bankruptcy. Although she didn't know that much about it, she decided to talk to a lawyer to find out more. After hearing what had happened, the attorney referred her to a specialist in securities law. Arbitrations began against the broker and the brokerage firm for selling Mrs. Perkins investments that were unsuitable for her situation.

This real-life situation didn't end at this point. However, in this chapter I've told enough of the story to ask the question, "Who's to blame?" To most, the obvious answer is the broker. He sold those investment products to Mrs. Perkins. The brokerage firm who employed him should be held responsible for its inappropriate advice. The brokerage firm will claim that Mrs. Perkins had full disclosure on all the partnerships and the financial strength of the insurance companies, and that she was greedy in trying to make more than a safe return. She participated in the process, and agreed to go ahead with the plan. From a legal viewpoint, both sides can make their case. Sure, the broker was a bit too aggressive with this particular client. Actually, the client did win an award in the real-world example I used. However, let's face it. Unless you are in the legal profession, you don't live your life to win a case in court. The last thing Mrs. Perkins wanted to do was to go to arbitration. She was only worried about buying food, paying her living expenses, and getting out of this mess with the ability to survive financially.

Wouldn't it have been a lot easier to have avoided getting into this problem in the first place? Investors would do themselves a favor by concentrating some of their efforts on keeping themselves out of situations like this. Let's examine the story once more, looking at decision points that impact the outcome.

Try to Make Money, Then Pay Your Taxes

First, there's the part about saving taxes. I can't say that I have ever met a person who tries to pay more taxes. It is logical and healthy to take advantage of every tax break. However, *it is not healthy to become obsessed with tax reduction to the point where the safety, liquidity, or economic sense of an investment portfolio is affected.* Mrs. Perkins should have considered the possibility that the investments the new broker was recommending were less liquid, and, if things turned sour, she would be in trouble. This would have given her a solid reason to say no.

Another reason one should be more oriented toward investment quality rather than tax advantages is our government. Congress has shown itself to be fickle and meddlesome when it comes to tax law. It is constantly trying to fiddle with some part of the economy or come up with more tax revenues. If an investment is based on tax breaks that Congress decides to eliminate, the investment may look very poor indeed. For this reason, I remain cautious about most tax-advantaged investments.

Paying taxes can be looked at as the glass that's half empty or half full. Even if you are in a 50 percent tax bracket, for every extra dollar you make, you get to keep 50 cents. Many investors concentrate so much on the negative aspects of paying 50 cents to the government on that extra dollar, they lose sight of the 50 cents they put in their own pocket. I choose to look at the glass that is half full and play a game each year called "Let's pay more taxes this year than I paid last year." If I do have a higher tax bill this year, then I remember that it is because I have had a more profitable year and I pay my tax bill. Try it next April. You may find that you enjoy playing my tax game as well.

Read the Legal Paperwork

The second decision point Mrs. Perkins had was to *take the responsibility for purchasing the investment.* Over the years, hundreds of investors have told me they haven't read the legal prospectus or disclosure given to them before they invested. Why? Perhaps they didn't understand it or they didn't have the time to consider it. Maybe they were lazy, or they simply trusted their advisor. But by not reading the legal document and fully understanding it, the investor fails to take responsibility for the decision. That responsibility has then been delegated to someone else. This leaves the investor at another person's mercy.

Remember, the laws require that investors receive proper disclosure before they invest. These laws were written in an attempt to protect the investor from scams and misrepresentations. The investor ends up paying for this protection in lower returns on his or her investment. As long as one is paying for it, *why not take the time and trouble to read the disclosure and ask questions before making the investment?* It might save a lot of time and trouble later.

All Risks Are Not Created Equal

Mrs. Perkins made the decision to go forward with the investment because it seemed that she could make a little more money with the broker's new recommendations. This is a natural human tendency. But *in focusing on the reward, she forgot about the risk.* Each investment strategy carries its own level of risks.

There are many forms of risk. Markets can move up and down, creating market risk. The custodian holding the investment could default, creating potential risk of institutional failure. Bond and stock investors could face the risk of a company going bankrupt, creating credit risk. Investors could see world events move their investments rapidly up or down, which could be called volatility risk. The declining purchasing power of the dollar creates inflation or currency risk.

These are not risks the investor needs to dwell on. Most of these risks are either minimal or have little probability of occurring. Others are predictable and can be planned for. Unfortunately, just because they are minimal or predictable does not mean the investor should ignore them. Studying risk should be done with an open, balanced mind. Paranoia is not our goal here; realism is where we want to operate. How would I feel as a stock investor if the stock market went down 50 percent as it did back in 1973–74? Could I live with what happened in the Crash of '87, when most stock mutual funds went down over 20 percent? What would I do if my broker, bank, or savings and loan went bankrupt? What would happen to my bonds if the company that issued them defaulted on the payments? Would I feel comfortable with the investment if it started moving up or down by more than one percent each day? How would I react to a negative news article about a company whose stock I own?

This is real life. These things happen. Making believe that someone else is looking out for these risks is like out of sight, out of mind. This is the "Ignorance Is Bliss" approach to investing. Just because someone doesn't admit that these risks are real, doesn't mean they do not exist. On the other hand, it doesn't mean a person should dwell on them. These risks will affect each individual differently. A risk that one person might brush off might worry another individual. So the next time you consider switching to another investment for a higher return, realize that you probably are not dealing with exactly the same risk structure as the investment you are contemplating leaving. In addition, there may be costs in making the move to a new alternative. Make sure the switch is really worth it.

Some investors refuse to learn about various risks. They either don't want to face the risk or simply don't have the time to mess with it. For these investors, a second opinion is a must. If a doctor wanted to perform surgery, most patients would get a second opinion. If a financial advisor gives you a financial diagnosis, locate another financial advisor, not in any way compensated by the investment, and get a second opinion.

So, who's to blame for some of the investments you've made in the past? Think back to some disappointing deal that you bought. Then think all the way back to the beginning. Were there points along the way where you could have changed the outcome by deciding something differently? Did you have a plan for how to get out of the investment with a profit? Did you have an alternate plan for how to get out if things went badly? Did you read the legal paperwork? Did you balance your mental state and give yourself some worst-case scenarios in order to remain unemotional about buying the investment? Did you understand all the risks? Asking some tough questions of yourself will help you avoid some future investing mistakes, so you won't ever have to ask the question, "Who's to blame?"

Chapter Five

Keep Your Money from the Person Managing It!

Over the years, I have read with interest the details about some of the great financial con jobs that have occurred. My purpose in studying them is to avoid getting sucked into one of them myself. I am not trying to scare investors away from managed futures with the following example. What happened to Dr. Jones could be true of any type of investment. Pay attention to where the actual cash is. There's something here for everyone.

Dr. Jones, a dentist in Phoenix, was attending a cocktail party one weekend when he happened to run into a fellow dentist, Dr. Kent. The subject turned to their pension plans. Dr. Kent was having some unbelievable success with her plan. She had invested a few months before with a local money manager, Wine and Rose, Inc. She understood very little about the operation, but another dentist had referred her to them. Dr. Kent thought that her associate knew what he was doing. Her latest statement showed her investment up 20 percent in three months. Dr. Jones' interest skyrocketed. He asked for, and received, the phone number of Wine and Rose, Inc.

He got some information on the investment. Wine and Rose, Inc. was apparently a commodity pool operator and trading advisor that invested in "more conservative financial futures." The track record was amazingly steady, and had produced "over 40 percent returns in the last 12 months." Dr. Jones decided to go in with 25 percent of his pension plan, and sent the money to Wine and Rose, Inc.

After three months and about a 15 percent return, Dr. Jones was impressed. After meeting with his pension administrator, he decided to up the investment to 50 percent of his plan. He looked forward to receiving his monthly statement and seeing how much he was making.

Then, one day it was all over the evening news. Federal marshals had closed down Wine and Rose, Inc. and impounded all its documents. Apparently they were falsifying monthly statements, and there was a suspicion that most of the investors' assets were in a private account somewhere in Singapore. The National Futures Association was investigating the matter, and was probably going to turn it over to the Commodity Futures Trading Commission. Charges would be filed against both Mr. Wine and Mr. Rose.

Dr. Jones' plans for early retirement flew away with the news report. Now he was missing 50 percent of his pension plan. The Department of Labor was considering examining the plan's investment policy to see if Dr. Jones, as the plan's trustee, had been prudent in investing the plan's assets. What a mess!

You might think that this is not an investment that an average investor would consider purchasing. Guess again. When the real-life story ended, over $15 million, invested by hundreds of normal people, were missing. One partner of Wine and Rose was missing; the other had been arrested on embezzlement and fraud charges. Let's analyze this example and see where the investor could have changed the outcome.

If It Sounds Too Good to Be True, It Probably *Is* Too Good to Be True

Dr. Jones found an investment that had tremendous potential. He could have hired someone to check out the investment. Finding an individual with the right experience and knowledge to properly check out the investment would have been difficult, but the tremendous potential would have justified the work. Certified public accountants know the tax laws, but sometimes are short on investment experience. Lawyers can read contracts, but frequently know little about investing. The National Futures Association information line in Chicago might have given Dr. Jones some ideas on how to check out an investment like this if he had called. Trade associations of reputable advisors might have been able to suggest a way to audit or check out the investment. If an investment has very high potential, do your homework! It would have been simple for Dr. Jones to go to Wine and Rose, Inc. and ask for copies of custodian statements to verify the great track record. Of course, those statements would not have been there, and Wine and Rose, Inc. would have been avoided. Perhaps Wine and Rose, Inc. could have faked the custodian documents. A simple call to the custodian would have verified that the trades that Wine and Rose, Inc. were making were not real. The point is, *if the investment is that good, then check it out three times as much,* because something may very well be wrong. Ask the manager how you can verify the track record's authenticity. Any reputable manager or a hired due diligence expert should be able and willing to prove it to you.

Don't Give Your Money to the Person Managing It

Another decision point for Dr. Jones was when he had to write his check directly to Wine and Rose, Inc. *Do not have your money at the firm that is managing your money.* This simple, but effective, rule drastically reduces your chances of being taken by a con job. For example, when opening a mutual fund account, you make out the check to the mutual fund's custodian, not to the investment advisor managing the fund. There is a separation of the person holding the money and the person making the investment decisions.

If an advisor has possession of your actual money, then he has the ability to invest it or to walk with it. There may be little or no restrictions preventing him from embezzling it. However, if the money that your advisor is managing is sitting at a different custodian, then the advisor cannot easily steal the money. This is fairly standard practice in the mutual fund industry, where large funds are custodied at bank custodians and the investment manager is in a separate company. In this type of setup, the custodian and the manager can cross-check each other. Obviously, these entities should be independent to keep the cross-checking meaningful. The moment Dr. Jones found he had to write a check to Wine and Rose, Inc., who was also going to manage the money, he should have walked away from the investment.

This simple rule would have kept investors out of the real estate fiascoes in recent years, the oil scams of the 1980s, and most commodity and option rip-offs. Investors would also have been protected from some malicious private investment deals.

My rule for separating the person holding the cash from the person making the investment decisions would also prevent investors from leaving their money at a brokerage firm and then following the broker's advice routinely. Brokers have, for many years, been providing financial advice and then have been paid for executing transactions. In these situations, the brokers are supposed to be holding the cash and the clients are supposed to be making the investment decisions. If that were the case, my rule would not be violated and I would find that situation acceptable. However, clients frequently agree to a broker's recommendations with a passive "Sounds good to me." The broker is not legally managing the account. However, with the client agreeing to everything, the broker is, in reality, managing the account. This implies that the same person holding the cash is also making the investment decisions. This is the way many investors currently have their accounts handled. The discerning investor should wonder, "Is the broker recommending this because it is appropriate, or is he selling me something to make a commission?"

I would prefer to see brokers compensated by fees, not by commissions. Unfortunately, that is not the way the world currently works. There is a trend in the brokerage community toward packaged products with trailing fees for the broker, and managed stock accounts with wrap fees and no commissions. As more of these approaches become commonplace, this potential conflict of both holding a client's assets and providing transaction advice will fade from the marketplace. An added benefit to the brokerage community would be a reduction in legal expenses defending churning cases where brokers buy and sell rapidly to produce large amounts of sales commissions. If brokers did not receive sales commissions, there would be no incentive to churn an account, which would drastically reduce the justification for litigation.

Separation of the manager from the money is very important. *Take an inventory of your assets, and try to decide where you have ample cross-checks and where you don't.* Cross-checks are simply ways of having the person holding the cash and the person making the investment decisions monitor each other. Another option is to have a trustworthy third party watch over investment decisions.

If you have some money with a financial manager and have little or no cross-checks on the assets, ask for routine accounting audits to verify the returns or watch those investments closely for potential problems. You might also consider diversifying some of your money to investments with a safer structure to prevent someone from leaving town with all your money.

Chapter Six

Give Yourself
Balanced Scenarios

Successful investors, all other things being equal, must have a different state of mind than unsuccessful investors. In Jack Schwager's two books, *Market Wizards* and *The New Market Wizards*, there are interviews with many very successful investors. A number of them would be considered legends. But every one of them is different in what and how they trade. The frustrated investor is left with the question, "What's the common ingredient that makes these successful investors different from me?" All these traders are persistent. Most carefully monitor and limit their risk to comfortable levels, using money management techniques. They all have learned a great deal from their mistakes. However, let's look at another important characteristic common to every one of them: the human mind.

Mr. Downs was reading at home one night after dinner. A phone call from a broker cold-calling new clients interrupted his reading. It was Johnny Sharp, calling to introduce himself and his firm, Cold Callers, Inc. He didn't have any specific recommendations. But if his firm came up with a good idea, would Mr. Downs be interested? Mr. Downs thought a second about the bonus he would soon be receiving, and decided that perhaps he should start an investing program. He was not getting any younger, and hadn't really put very much away for retirement. So he said, "Why not?"

A week went by, and Mr. Downs got his bonus. That very night, almost on cue, Johnny Sharp called with his first idea. A new public offering by a small company, Anything Goes, Inc., was coming out in a few days. The company wanted to mass-market widgets. This was a new concept, since widgets were generally sold in smaller, independent stores. If their market projections for widgets were even half right, the stock was likely to triple in value. The dollar signs appeared in front of Mr. Downs' eyes. He had an instant vision of the stock tripling, his spouse and friends admiring his investment prowess, his financial security increasing, and his retirement program starting up with a flash. His vision of the future felt good, and his excitement level increased. He decided to go ahead with the investment. Johnny Sharp agreed to put in an order for 500 shares.

The public offering came in a few days. Johnny was on the phone that night with news that the offering was hot and oversubscribed. The stock had first traded at $1 per share; by the end of the day it had shot up to $2. A chill of excitement raced through Mr. Downs' body as his dreams materialized with the good news. Everything was going just fine. His instincts about the deal had turned out right, and he was even more excited about the prospects for tomorrow. Mr. Downs asked Johnny if he would call him the next day at work to keep tabs on his investments. Johnny agreed that would be a good idea, as the markets were moving fast and they might have to make some decisions about where to take profits.

The next day, the stock went to $3 per share. Johnny was on the phone to Mr. Downs explaining that $3 per share was their research department's objective for the stock. Perhaps he should lock in his profits. That sounded like a good idea to Mr. Downs. The gain would then be realized and become tangible. He could taste the investing victory about to unfold. He gave the go-ahead, and they made the trade. It was sweet. This was easy money. Another few trades like this and maybe he could seriously consider retiring early.

After taking his wife out to celebrate, Mr. Downs came home to find the phone ringing. Johnny was on the line talking about another deal that was coming out next week that looked good. Actually, it might have even more potential than the stock they had just sold for a profit. Mr. Downs said to count him in, and ordered 2,000 shares. He might as well commit a significant amount to such a promising deal.

I hope I'm not becoming too predictable with these stories, but you can probably guess what happened next. Mr. Downs couldn't wait for the stock to be issued. The offering was weak, and the stock immediately began to slip. The investment banker tried to stabilize the price, but it never went any higher. Weeks of waiting went by with no appreciable chance to get out with a profit. Johnny called with other deals, but Mr. Downs had most of his money tied up in this one issue. Eventually, the company ran into difficulty and went bankrupt. Mr. Downs' dreams became nightmares. He had to forget about retiring early. His friends said they had told him so. His wife's nagging seemed a little more intense. The pressures of his job seemed to weigh him down, as he envisioned himself working there forever. Mr. Downs was now in a very frustrated state of mind. It's amazing how one invest-ment can make such a change in a person's mental state, but it fre-quently happens to investors.

Keep a Balanced State of Mind

Let's analyze this example with a focus on mental states. *The major difference between successful investors and unsuccessful investors is their mental approach to investing.* Mr. Downs is a very typical human being. When things were going well, he was happy and excited, and projected that emotional high into the future. Alternately, he became frustrated when things took a turn for the worse. He projected that frustration into the future, and could only see the dark side of things. Since you are just a casual observer to this example, you probably were in a detached state of mind while reading it. You might have even jumped to conclusions about how the story would end. You were creating the different investment scenarios before you read them. The detached state of mind you were probably in gave you more ability to come up with a variety of possibilities. Mr. Downs, in his emotional state, could not see the alternatives.

Successful investors have a state of mind that can best be summed up in the word "balanced." When a person becomes emotional or unbalanced, his mind goes into a restricted state. This gets the adren-aline flowing, creates possible excitement or frustration, and limits the investor's mental choices. The successful investor will stay more un-emotional and detached from investing, perhaps looking at the process as an interesting game. Others would call it a challenge or brain tease. The successful investor doesn't get seduced into the emotional roller coaster mental state that characterizes so many frustrated investors. Can you put yourself into a detached state of mind the next time you are considering an investment?

Watching the Movie of Life

A technique that works for me is to think of investing as a movie I'm watching. This concept could be applied to your entire life as well, but

41

for now let's concentrate on investing. If you can watch yourself managing your portfolio instead of consciously participating in the investing process, you will achieve a certain degree of detachment. Instead of talking to your broker, watch yourself talking to your broker. Instead of trying to understand an investment, watch yourself trying to understand the investment.

The reason watching the movie works for me is that I can watch myself getting excited or frustrated and take steps to do something about it. People who are very emotional about investing do not realize that they are emotional. In a highly emotional state, investors have more difficulty logically and objectively evaluating alternatives. *If they could see themselves becoming emotional, they could delay making a decision until they are in a less emotional condition, or choose to change their mental state.*

A noted investment author once suggested not making an investment decision while the markets were open. While this initially sounded like letting important time pass, I later realized that he was suggesting that investors wait until the heat of the moment has passed and emotions subside before making an investment decision.

Give Yourself Alternate Scenarios

Now that you're thinking with a balanced state of mind, it's easy to give yourself balanced scenarios. *Always give your mind the possible good and bad of an investment idea.* This helps maintain your balanced state. You won't get too excited when things are going well, nor frustrated when things don't work out.

You can always develop a negative scenario with any investment. For a ridiculous example, let's say you want to put your life savings into U.S. Treasury Bills. I might argue that you should diversify. You might say, "How can I go wrong with an investment backed by the U.S. government?" Well, let's get imaginative. The deficit continues to get bigger to the point that there's a public outcry. Congress looks around for the money and realizes that if they could just skip some interest payments, they could start catching up with the deficit. Without any national debt, the U.S. government would have positive cash flow and could spend more money on programs they can't afford. They decide that most of the holders of Treasury Bills are wealthy people and foreigners. So, in an insane moment (Congress has these from time to time), Congress decides to forego the next payment on all the public debt, including reduced payments for all T-Bills. T-Bills immediately sell off, and no interest flow occurs on the investment if held to maturity. Is this possible? Absolutely! Is it likely? Probably not. But now that we've described a possible way that Congress might change the value of your investments, is it prudent to put all your money into T-Bills?

There is always a worst-case scenario you can develop for an investment. For a stock, it might be a bankruptcy or a market crash. A bond might default on the interest payments. Changed tax laws could affect your real estate holdings, municipal bonds, or insurance investments. If you cannot come up with a worst-case scenario, a reputable broker, financial planner, or investment advisor can help you consider some. Your goal in developing balanced scenarios is to keep your mind balanced with both good and bad possibilities. It then becomes more logical to have stop-loss points to prevent runaway losses. This will keep you thinking clearly, and give you mental choices in making logical investment decisions.

Chapter Seven ──────

────── If It Isn't Broken, Don't Fix It!

I've already given you some thoughts about people who are unabashed optimists when investing. They see the glass as half full. On the other hand, some investors see the glass as half empty. These people spend much of their time looking at what is wrong with a situation. This philosophy spills over into their investing. Let's examine the case of Jim Franklin.

Jim was a cautious investor. He was not the type who rushed into anything. His financial planner in Atlanta, Neil Granite, told Jim about something called a mutual fund timing program. This timing program moved money between mutual funds based on trends measured by computer models. During strong up markets, the timing program would struggle to keep up with the market, but turn in a good return. During strong down markets, the program would move the funds to money markets preserving the client's assets and drastically outperforming the market. During sideways markets, the program would jump in when the market moved up, then jump out when the up move proved short-lived, in the process taking modest losses and underperforming the market. For a market cycle, the program looked like it had the possibility of a 2 percent edge over the market, with a risk structure 35 percent lower than the market's normal risk.

Jim researched these statistics, and then looked at several mutual fund timers. The market was moving up nicely during the period in which he was doing his research. This gave him confidence in the strength of these programs. Finally, Jim decided to invest his moneys with two different mutual fund timers.

One timing company immediately moved the money into the market, going with the current trend without waiting for any new indications on the market. It was their policy to do this with new clients. The other company decided to wait for the next full buy signal to jump in, since they considered this to be less risky. This was their policy with new investors. Both companies had fine track records and strong operations, but their strategies differed on this particular policy.

Jim started monitoring the investments he'd made. The market continued up for some time. The advisor that had jumped in immediately started looking very good. The advisor in cash started lagging badly.

This frustrated Jim, and he called the second advisor to chew him out and to encourage him to get into the market. The advisor politely told Jim that the reward-to-risk of the market was not as good now as it had been when the rest of his clients had bought into the market, and that waiting patiently for the next signal would be prudent. Jim's frustration grew as he saw himself missing out on the market's move with some of his moneys.

Then the market went into a sideways period. In line with their strategies, both advisors entered the market on buy signals and exited on sell signals, but each incurred losses as market trends went nowhere. The first advisor had built up some profits, and was giving some back. The second advisor had not jumped in initially, and, therefore, was now losing money. Both advisors were following their specified plan to the letter. With small overall losses, Jim was like a pressure cooker about to explode. He was furious with the second manager for missing some of the up move. Looking back, even he knew the market was strong, and certainly an expert wouldn't have missed out on the move. The first manager, after some initial profits, was now giving them all up. Adding up both managers, Jim was behind and heading down. From time to time he'd call the managers and give them a piece of his mind. They would calmly explain that they were following their programs precisely, and that over time the returns and the risk reduction would be there.

Each morning, Jim would look at the newspaper and become angry. Each monthly statement brought more bad news. Finally, it was too much. He decided that all those people who said timing doesn't work must have been right. Jim fired the managers, and put the money into a money market account until he could decide what to do with it.

It's Okay to Lose

It amazes me how often investors buy an investment or get into a managed program on the basis of an excellent five- or 10-year track record, only to jump out four months later, during a losing period. All track records will have periods of great success. They will also have periods of losses. This may sound cynical, but a track record without any losses might be about to have one. Check these out twice as much.

Losses are a part of making money. It's okay to take a loss. It's not that profits are good and losses are bad. Expecting to make only gains without ever taking a loss is a little like trying to breathe in without ever breathing out. Gains and losses are both part of the process of investing. Jim's decision to jump in when he did dictated that he would see some gains before seeing some losses. Had he started the programs a month earlier, he would have seen losses first, then gains, then losses. It doesn't make any difference to the successful investor who knows that both gains and losses are part of successful investing. Given the type of market conditions Jim invested in, both managers did as you might expect. The plan was not broken. Jim's frustration was inappropriate. He should have continued to retain both managers an feel comfortable about his long-term strategy.

Cut Your Losses Short

I am not saying that there isn't a point where an investor has to cut his losses short and run. You should be able to decide when a program is not working for you. You also need to decide when it's just a tough market and wait out the next big move. The easiest way to monitor your investment program is to write down some expected characteristics before investing. (The next chapter covers monitoring in great detail.) If you don't know enough about the investment or program, get help from a reputable financial advisor. *Write down the best-case scenario, the worst-case scenario, and the expected scenario. Write down how you expect the investment to perform during positive, negative, and sideways periods.* If you are working with a financial advisor, explore how your future investments are likely to perform during different types of markets. *Try to visualize what you expect to happen, and mentally rehearse how you will react to these periods.* Then, periodically, you can analyze your investment results and the scenarios

49

you've developed to see if what has happened so far is any surprise. If it is, maybe you have grounds for moving your investment to another area. If what has happened so far fits the profile you've outlined, then it isn't broken. So don't fix it!

Chapter Eight

The Art of Monitoring an Investment

I call monitoring an art instead of a science for good reason: I don't know any way to reduce it to just numbers, although many try to do exactly that. For each investor, monitoring will take different forms. For some, looking at monthly statements is fine. Others glance at their investments in the daily paper. A few look at their realized gains and losses (Schedule D) on their year-end tax forms. All these forms of monitoring may be fine for an individual. Let's look at an example.

Frank Lee was a successful executive in Orlando, Florida. Frank decided to retire, hire a money manager to manage his retirement portfolio, and enjoy his golden years. With the help of a financial planner, John Benton, Frank selected a money manager, to manage a conservative stock portfolio for himself and his wife.

Things got off to a great start. The portfolio was up about 20 percent in the first six months. Imagine the surprise when the money manager received a frantic call from Mr. Benton that the client was thinking of closing the account. The manager called the client and calmed him down, promising to meet with him sometime in the next two weeks when he was in town.

Frank Lee and his wife met the manager at Mr. Benton's office. Frank told the manager he just couldn't take it anymore. He realized that the account was up and he was making money. He realized that the program he was in was a long-term program. However, he was worried when he looked at the paper each morning and saw his investment go up and down in value. Despite his portfolio's increase, he was concerned about his health and the pressure he felt when he read the morning paper. The manager offered an easy solution: cancel the subscription to the morning paper. Frank understood the suggestion, but thought he would probably worry anyway. He felt the only solution to his problem was to invest in CDs at his local savings and loan. Only then would he be protected from the whims of the markets.

The manager was fired, and Mr. Lee went to the savings and loan. With a CD as his portfolio, Mr. Lee was relaxed, and started to enjoy his retirement. Then his savings and loan went bankrupt. Frank and his wife had no access to his funds until the Federal Savings and Loan Insurance Corporation (FSLIC) reviewed the books and decided how to protect investors. While the regulators went to work, Frank started worrying again. A few weeks later, a fatal heart attack ended his worrying.

What does this sad story teach us about the art of monitoring an investment program? Let's review some key mistakes that Mr. Lee made along the way.

Pick a Reasonable Time Period

Mr. Lee decided to monitor his investments daily. After all, he was retired and had the time to do so. He wanted this monitoring to give him some purpose in retirement. Part of his mind decided it would fill even more of his time if he worried about his investments all day. This is a good example of how the mind can give you exactly what you *really* want, rather than what you *think* you want.

Does it make any sense to monitor a managed stock account daily? I don't think so. Even though I have computers that keep track of our positions, and I have to manage those positions daily, I only look at monthly results to track the success or failure of the programs. Even then, I have to average many months to truly appreciate how the investment is performing in its respective market. *A single day doesn't say much about the performance of an investment strategy.* But remember, any single day could be significant enough to warrant action by the investor. *The point is that the time frame should be long enough to ignore the random noise of shorter-term movements, and yet short enough to allow the investor to take appropriate action.* If you want to be efficient in monitoring your investments, give some thought to how often you'll look at results. Then stick to your plan.

Observe the Environment

Before monitoring an investment, I look at the general investing climate. For example, if the stock market were down 5 percent for the month and a managed stock program were down 3 percent on average, I would be delighted. If the market were up 10 percent and the portfolio were up only 5 percent, I would start to get concerned. If the portfolio were to lag the market for a 12-month period, I would be very concerned, unless this was done with a lot less risk than the market. Saying that making profits is good and losing is bad is an oversimplification.

A broker once told me, "We sell bottom line and peace of mind." That's a good way for most investors to monitor. Bottom line is fine to analyze. However, when you have that urge to quit an investment program, it's a lack of peace of mind that is driving your decision. *Take a look at the investing environment to gain a better perspective on what your investment has faced.* In the previous chapter, I recommended writing down what you expect from an investment in a best-case, worst-case, and expected-case format. In monitoring, you can ask the question, "Is the investment behaving as I expected?" If it is, go on to other activities. If not, then it's time to find out why the investment is not performing as expected and decide on possible actions you might take with the investment. You might want to move on to something else, change the way the investment is managed, or alter your perceptions of what is normal for the investment and stay with it.

Understand How Your Investment Performs in Various Environments

It is also important to understand enough about how your investment is managed to determine its success in any single environment. For instance, if you are trend-following the market in a mutual fund timing program and the market is in a sideways, choppy period, expect your program to take small losses. If you are in a runaway bull (up) market, you should expect a large positive return, but probably slightly behind that of the market. If a long-term bear (down) market occurs, expect to spend a lot of time in money markets with small positive returns, drastically outperforming the declining market. Understanding how your investment strategy matches up to different scenarios gives you a better perspective on whether or not things are going as you would expect them to go.

Every Investment has Risk

Frank Lee thought that by getting rid of stocks he got rid of risk as well as his worries. He decided that there was no risk in a CD at a savings and loan. Yet every investment has some risk. Frank substituted credit risk for market risk. I am not saying that either of these risks is more important. Some investors might not wish to have any market risk, and, for them, CDs may be very appropriate. However, it is important to acknowledge that some risk exists with everything and face it, rather than ignore it. Ignoring risk may bring you peace of mind, but that peace of mind may be misguided.

You can't hide from risk. Remember, *the greatest risk of all is the unwillingness to take a risk.* Unless you take some risk, you have a 100 percent chance of accomplishing nothing.

Navigate the River of Investments

St. Louis has been my home for over 20 years. Missouri has a number of smaller rivers where you can go "floating" down the river in a canoe and enjoy some of beautiful countryside. We usually use two-person canoes. One person sits in front looking ahead and the other person sits in back using a paddle as a rudder. This arrangement reminds me of a financial advisor and an investor. The financial advisor can point out obstacles or opportunities ahead, but is hard-pressed to do very much about it unless the investor steers himself or herself toward the opportunity or out of the way of trouble.

The river of investing flows one way. When you're floating in the direction of the current of the financial markets, all you have to do is relax and enjoy the ride. When you get to the financial rapids, and

It's more complicated than that!!

money is being made too quickly, you have to steer around potential obstacles and stay out of trouble. If you decide to try to go upstream against the market, you have to work like crazy to make any progress. It's like trying to make money in stocks in a market that's going lower. You work hard just to stay even. I would no more expect to make money owning stocks during the Crash of '87, than I would expect to be able to paddle upstream successfully in the rapids.

So, think about the river when monitoring your investment results. If you've had the current going your way, don't get too pleased with yourself. There may be rough water ahead. If you've been fighting the current, don't get too frustrated if progress has been slow. Your efforts will be rewarded when the river flows your way.

Chapter Nine

Chasing the Hot Track Record

One of the most common mistakes frustrated investors make is chasing the hot track record. Although it defies logic at first, let me suggest that, for most investors, picking a manager with the best track record may be a frustrating way to invest moneys. Let's poke some fun at Tom Winter.

Tom was a typical novice investor. He saved up some money in 1980. He decided he should look into investing, so he actively talked to friends and brokers about investments. Nothing seemed exciting to him until he met Mike Robbins. Mike was a talker. He loved to pass on gossip, tips, and investment concepts. He loved to talk about investments. It was his passion. He seemed like an investment genius to Tom Winter. Mike told him how much money people were making in gold. Gold had recently moved up from $200 per ounce to about $750 per ounce. Investors buying gold bullion were reporting gains of 275 percent! This caught Tom's attention. He would like to make that kind of return. Who wouldn't want some of that action?

A few days later, Tom entered the gold market. He ended up paying $800 per ounce, but that didn't concern him, since the market was so strong. It would be at $1,000 per ounce within a month. In addition, Mike Robbins told him the experts said that gold could go to $3,000 per ounce within the next four years.

Gold did not go to $3,000 or even $1,000. Almost on cue, it nosedived. A few years went by. Tom was patient, but not a bit pleased about gold's continued decline. Tom ran into Mike Robbins again. Mike was excited about the returns coming out of a manager specializing in small stocks. Tom took the manager's number and called him. Returns of over 30 percent per year for the past three years sure sounded a lot better than watching gold sink lower and lower. Tom sold the gold and hired the manager.

About then, the market for small secondary stocks peaked. The new manager did all he could to stem the losses, but he couldn't work miracles. While the larger companies in the Dow Jones average continued to make new highs, the stocks that Tom owned fell. However, Tom continued to be patient and believe that his new manager would make a comeback. He vowed to stick with it.

A few years later, the story repeated itself with junk bonds that were hot, then fell apart with the Drexel collapse. The leveraged buyout manager followed next in 1987. Tom found himself owning an assortment of special situations during the Crash of '87. A few years later, the story repeated itself again with a managed commodity account with a hot manager that went cold. Tom then moved on to a mutual fund that was managing billions and had the number one track record over the past 10 years. The fund went nowhere and was eventually below where Tom had bought it.

Tom Winter was a defeated man. It seemed that every time he heard about a great investment, it turned on him. He was always out of step with the markets. After 10 years of having the investment world put it to him, he was a very frustrated investor.

This story may sound familiar, since this is a common problem among investors. If you haven't personally suffered through a period like this, chances are you know someone who has. Let's look at the lesson this story can teach us.

Crowd Psychology Is Usually Wrong

It may be very hard to resist an investment idea when everyone else is making money on it. But if you want to reduce your frustrations, that's exactly what you must do. Adam Smith, in his best-selling book, *The Money Game,* said that the best book he ever read about investor psychology was *Extraordinary Popular Delusions and the Madness of Crowds.* The title tells it all. I have noticed that when we have an unusually high number of new clients signing up, that investment program is ready for a setback. The opposite is also true. We have the most clients leaving an investment program exactly as that program is ready for a profitable move. We could almost create an indicator out of the "net clients coming-minus-going" to call market tops and bottoms.

Successful investor Jim Rogers has described successful investing as a process of waiting until you find an investment that looks like cash lying over in the corner of the room, ignored by everyone. All you have to do is go over and pick it up. Investing legends John Templeton and Warren Buffet are known for their technique of finding good value, buying it, and then patiently and profitably waiting for it to be discovered by other investors willing to drive prices to fair value.

When you hear about the same hot track record from many sources, it is best to detach yourself from it and look for other opportunities currently being ignored. Some of the best investment ideas are those that are boring, unattractive, or uninteresting to most of the investing public.

Chapter Ten ───

─── ## Is This a Good
Deal or What?

The previous chapter discussed the problems with chasing the latest investment craze. It's too easy to buy an investment right before it tops out. However, as is often the case in the world of investments, the other extreme can frustrate the investor, as the following example shows.

Brian Sloane was a successful real estate developer in California. Over two decades, he had designed, built, purchased, and sold countless office complexes. In the process, he had built a substantial net worth. He was respected in his field as one of the high-end developers in the city.

But the late 1980s and the early 1990s brought an end to easy money in real estate. Brian was careful to avoid the pitfalls and maintained a successful, though downsized operation. He concentrated on management of existing buildings, and searched high and low for a "good deal" to buy. For years it seemed that none existed. He calculated that with changes in the tax laws and an oversupply of office space, it would take years for the market to get interesting again.

Brian wasn't one to sit around wasting time. He decided to spend some of his efforts fooling around with a few stocks. Well, fool around he did. After losing money on a few storytime stocks from the broker, he decided to get serious about investing. After all, he wasn't bringing in much from the real estate business. His portfolio should be managed to give him some upside potential.

He decided to approach stocks in the same way he tried to buy real estate. First, he scanned the popular financial dailies and weeklies, looking for indications that a stock had sold off significantly. Articles that talked about a quality company that had announced some temporary hard times but was ready to come back were particularly attractive. He waited until a company's stock price was down 10 or 20 percent and bought it cheap. He looked for "buying opportunities," as he called them. It was actually quite easy to find a number of these buying opportunities at any point in time, so he could afford to be selective. He checked out the fundamentals of companies and received reports from his broker on each company. He also bought significant amounts of each stock so that his costs were minimized. He concentrated on technology stocks, since he figured they would move the fastest and produce the best returns.

A few years later, Brian noticed something interesting about his stocks. Some of his purchases had been brilliant. He would wait patiently, until he saw a buying opportunity present itself. Then, he would put a limit order just under the current price and pick it up cheap. Within weeks, the price would move back up, producing a quick profit.

Other purchases seemed like good buying opportunities at the time. Brian would wait, buy them cheap, and then watch them drift lower. One quality stock actually gave him three different buying opportunities from $35 down to $19 per share. He bought more shares all the way down, adding to his losses.

For a while, everything seemed fine. The stocks that went up produced some flashy, quick profits. The stocks that went down seemed to languish. Overall, the portfolio's value wasn't up much, but Brian seemed to be able to lock in some good profits.

Eventually, Brian acquired larger positions in the stocks that provided more buying opportunities and sold the stocks that seemed to race upward. His portfolio had more dogs and fewer stars and was going nowhere. Just like real estate, he had bought his stocks at great prices. He searched for the magic solution, but it was not to be found. Brian became frustrated with his portfolio and wondered what to do next.

A Good Deal Can Get Even Better

The first lesson we can learn from Brian is that simply buying an investment at a low price isn't sufficient to guarantee success. If an investment or a managed account is headed lower, the only limit to its decline is when the price hits zero and you lose all your investment. A "buying opportunity" to one person may be outrageously priced to another.

The only fair deal is the current price in the marketplace for the investment. Each day buyers and sellers come together and exchange investments. They both feel they're getting a fair deal, or no trades would occur. I'm not saying that you can't find attractive investments by doing your homework. But remember that an investment that looks cheap might be on its way to becoming even cheaper.

Reporters Are Just Doing Their Job

Brian found many of his stocks by noticing stories in the daily and weekly financial publications about companies with rebound potential after a sharp loss. It might be a leading software company that was facing competition and had to cut prices, but had slashed staff and held on to its market share. Perhaps it was a story about a company with a major new product that faced a delayed government approval, but still expected to move ahead soon. Every article gave investors the hope that things would be back on track and that the future looked great.

The investor should be well aware of the typical process and motivations behind these articles before using them to make investment decisions. A newspaper's or magazine's primary goal is to sell subscriptions. It does this by producing a quality publication on time with a variety of stories that its readership will find interesting.

The reporter is either assigned articles to write or comes up with some of his or her own with the approval of an editor. In most cases, these articles are written to garner the acceptance of their readership, thereby selling more copies of whatever is being written. No one logically looking at the financial publications available on the newsstand would expect anything else. It's not bad that the publications appeal to their readership. If they didn't, they wouldn't exist very long in this very competitive area.

So, what would you expect would sell more papers? They could write a story about a company going down the drain, then be accused of being too heavy-handed by the company and destroy the hope of all the investors that own the company's stock. They could just as easily write a story about how the company is getting its act together, and give the company's investors an uplifting pep talk. Hope springs eternal, as they say. Human beings love to hope for the best. Hopeful pieces will sell more papers than negative ones, so that is what you will read. A few years back, a major brokerage firm was "bullish on America." This advertising slogan would have more investor appeal than "We think America is in trouble." We all like to hope things get better, not worse.

Generally, reporters get their ideas from the world around them or questions and comments from readers. If a current event is getting people excited, they'll want to do a piece on it. When are investors the most excited? They are excited at market tops and bottoms. At market tops, you'll see all sorts of articles on why the market will go higher, because this is what investors want to read. They've already paid too much for their investment and they need the media's reassurance that they still might make money on their purchase.

At market bottoms, when all hope is gone, the last of the sellers liquidates his or her investment. During these periods, readers need reinforcement that they made the right choice in giving up on an investment. Articles might justify a continuation of the downtrend or reasons why a company is not going to make it.

You, the reader, have to be able to read the articles with a certain amount of detachment. You must realize or suspect the motivation behind the article. Is it a thinly disguised public relations piece for the company, rewritten by a reporter trying to meet a deadline? Is it an article simply reflecting the mood of the investing public, which is usually wrong? Could it be an article containing, facts and reasons for the market to go either up or down? Forming your own opinion is critical to good investing. Articles you read must provide facts, and you must try to prevent those articles from inappropriately coloring your opinions.

Let Your Gains Run—Cut Your Losses Short

The last thought I would share on Brian's investing story is the old trader's axiom: "Let your profits run and cut your losses short." Brian concentrated on buying stocks that had run down, hoping to see them rally and then to sell them out for a quick profit. He loaded up on stocks that went down from where he bought them and provided additional "buying opportunities." He was limiting his gains with the quick sales and letting his losses run with his additional purchases. This is the opposite of what makes sense in the markets.

Frequently, the best thing for an investor to do in a situation is to act in a way that will be most uncomfortable. For example, taking a loss is difficult at times. You have to admit failure, and nobody likes to do that. Taking a quick profit is fun and quite easy to do, but it does not let a winner run its course, providing the bigger profits you desire. My own attitude toward trading is to find a good investment, and hold it either the rest of my life or until it no longer should be held, whichever comes first. Realistically, investments will generally have their day in the sun, then rest for a while or fall out of favor. *If an investment you own is going against you, do not add to your losses by buying more of it.* Consider selling it and moving to other alternatives. *Hold on to those winners. They are sometimes hard to come by.*

Chapter Eleven

Beware of the
10-Year Track Record

I am often asked by investors, "What's the 10-year track record of this investment?" When a client is given the number for the average annualized return of the past 10 years, that number goes into the client's mind as if it were a fixed yield. The longer the track record, the more the client believes that the average return is reproducible. *The more you base your decisions just on track records, the more you set yourself up for frustration.*

Bill Ramsey decided to invest some of his extra dollars in a good, long-term mutual fund. He gathered copies of several magazines and reports from services that analyzed the performance of the universe of mutual funds available to investors. For convenience, these services sorted the performance so that Bill was able to see the top 10 performers over the past one, three, five, and 10 years.

Bill immediately noticed that one fund showed up on everyone's list. It was large and well-respected. The same manager had been with the fund since its inception. Its 10-year track record was +29 percent per year annualized. Bill thought to himself, "What am I doing with my money in CDs at 7 percent?" He immediately called the fund and invested.

The fund was listed in the local paper, so Bill started tracking it every day. The price moved quite a bit, but it seemed to be generally heading up, so everything looked good. By the end of the first month, Bill's account was up 4 percent, well on target to hit +30 percent by year's end. This went on a few months, with most of the returns on the upside. Then one day the market started to weaken. Bill noticed the price of his fund was down one percent in one day! He thought it must be a mistake, but, after calling the fund, he determined that it was true. For the next week, the market continued to weaken. Bill watched the price slip day after day. Another one percent-down day really started getting to him. A large amount of the earlier gain was now gone, and if the present trends were to persist, he would soon be behind on his investment.

Bill decided to call the fund to ask what had gone wrong. The manager answered that the market looked a little weak, and their stocks were hit a little harder than others since they had run up more during the previous up period. The manager tried to calm Bill down by saying that it was nothing to worry about. He said these moves happen all the time in the market, and if Bill stayed with it for the long term, he'd be fine.

Bill had enough! He decided that the manager must be trying to cover up for something, because the current performance was nowhere near the +29 percent per year track record that he had seen. He called back the fund and asked for his money. In a frustrated state of mind, Bill wondered where he would now invest.

This is another story that has been repeated all too frequently. Let's look at the story for some educational lessons.

Total Return Is Not Yield

Unless you are looking for a specific cash flow, never ask a stock manager, "What's the yield?" This is a tip-off that you are a rookie. Total return is the return on investment, including both the yield and the capital gains. Yield is just the interest or dividends that the investment pays. Most investors would be better served to study the total return rather than the yield, since this is the total bottom-line results they will receive.

For example, let's consider the case of an investor who buys a bond mutual fund and holds it for one year. He receives monthly interest checks that total a yield of 8 percent. However, the price of the bond mutual fund goes down 5 percent. This means the total return is roughly 3 percent (8 percent − 5 percent = 3 percent). If the investor spends all his interest payments and the total return is less than the yield every year, his investment would dwindle over future years.

If you take a 10-year annualized track record and split it into 12 equal segments for monthly return targets, you will find that you will soon be frustrated. *A long-term track record means a track record over many years. It is the combination of winning months, losing months, winning years, and losing years*. This is normal and expected. Why do investors analyze something with a 10-year track record, fill out all the paperwork, and then fire the manager in the first three months because he's lost them money? It's absurd.

Imagine Living with the Investment

Instead of locking into one number for the 10-year track record, I suggest "living with the investment." In other words, before you invest, get some data on the monthly returns and put a piece of paper over the results. Then look at one month at a time, moving the paper down to reveal the next period's performance. See if you feel comfortable with those ups and downs. Imagine you own it. How do those down months in the track record feel? If you are uncomfortable with the way an investment has moved in the past, forget the investment. It's liable to make you uncomfortable in the future.

Why Was the 10-Year Record So Good, and Is It Reproducible?

A lot can change over 10 years in today's world. Success attracts attention, and money will flow to successful managers. But these managers are also human, and cannot manage an infinite amount of money. Managers get sick, retire, or move on to other jobs, so the current manager may not be the same individual that created the track record you are buying. The fund's investment philosophy or trading approach may change even if the same manager has stayed with the fund. I have seen funds on the top 10 list with billions of dollars that generated much of their excess return back when they were less than $250 million. In case you don't know, it's a lot easier to manage $250 million that it is to manage billions. At that large size, instead of participating in the market, you move the market. Unless you look behind the 10-year track record, you may not notice dramatic changes in the investment's ability to reproduce in the future what it has generated in the past.

Make a Strategic Decision to Get into and out of an Investment

Bill, in our story, made a logical strategic decision to get into the fund. He looked at 10-year track records and, presumably, was hoping he would hold the fund for 10 years when he bought it. Then, when a period came along that didn't match his expectations, he made a tactical decision to get out of it. *It is more productive to develop a strategy to get out before getting in.* Then when it comes time to pull the plug on an investment, you are following a strategic plan, not just reacting emotionally.

Select Something a Little More Conservative Than You Think You Can Tolerate

Track records are only an accounting of historical results. You should remember that the legal disclaimer says, "Historical results do not imply future performance." However, everyone looks at them anyway. It is easy to dump a bunch of numbers into a computer and have it tell you the best track record. It is not so easy to dig into the investment and see what has changed over the past 10 years. It is also not so easy to look into the future and match the investment you are contemplating against your vision of the future. *Just because an investment hasn't done something in the past doesn't mean it can't do it in the future.*

If you investment has a 10 percent drawdown (down) period in its track record, and you are comfortable with a 10 percent down period, then you might be tempted to invest. A drawdown is a period of losses sustained in the market value of a portfolio, after which the portfolio recovers and hits new highs in market value. If slightly more than 10 percent down would cause you concern, then that investment may eventually make you nervous during a future losing period. Try to give yourself some psychological room. That way, if the investment has a particularly tough period to deal with, you can feel comfortable sticking with it. However, this is not an exact science. *Try to anticipate your lack of comfort with the investment. Try to look for something in the track record or management style that makes you nervous.* What you find may be what will cause you to sell in the future. You can then save yourself the frustration of one more unsuccessful investment.

Chapter Twelve —————

Diversify to
Your Comfort Level

Investors always want the best. This search for the best in investments implies that one investment is better than all the rest. This is why so many people read the top 10 rankings in the magazines or pay consultants to analyze the track records. "Nothing but the best for me," they say, or, "I deserve the best investment." Let's visit Sandy Moore in his pursuit of investment perfection.

Sandy was an engineer nearing retirement. He was very comfortable with numbers, since he had worked with them his entire career. It was natural for him to look at the numbers when selecting an investment. His plan was to create an investment program that he would manage after he received his lump-sum distribution from the company pension plan. He even started six months before the lump sum was available so he would have plenty of time to study the matter.

In disciplined, engineer fashion, Sandy went to the public library reference room and started studying various newsletters and reports on investment management services for the best investment. He also let brokers and financial planners know he was looking for something to do with his future pension distribution.

Sandy started reviewing various alternatives, and decided right away that he needed a plan for analyzing the multitude of numbers. He programmed his home computer to analyze various track records, simulate account value drawdowns, and report various measures of risk. After a few months of inputting various alternatives, a local manager, Computer Investing Unlimited, rose to the top of the list. Sandy visited the manager, and was impressed by the computerized operation and friendly, energetic staff.

The choice was simple. When the lump sum arrived, Sandy would invest in Computer Investing's managed growth stock program. The papers were finished, and Sandy executed his plan flawlessly.

Since Sandy had some time to monitor the investment he chose, he decided to create a variation of his computer program to track the performance of his new manager. He loaded the monthly values into the computer.

Some months were up and some were down. Sandy noticed that during one down month, the manager badly underperformed the market. He decided to meet with the manager to find out why this had occurred. The meeting at the manager's office was cordial and informative. Sandy left with a better appreciation of how difficult good investing is, and with a feeling that the management firm was doing all it could to deal with chaotic markets.

However, this started Sandy thinking. All his eggs were in this one basket. He'd better watch that basket very closely. He decided to monitor the portfolio daily. A computer database service was available to provide daily prices, so he subscribed and automated the portfolio tracking software.

The market started into a six-month slide that took the portfolio down about 11 percent. The drop was nothing unusual—quite slow and methodical. But Sandy started becoming very concerned. This was all the money he had for retirement. If it were gone, he would have to go back to work. He decided to take the money away from the manager and diversify his portfolio. Sandy started looking for additional investments, and moved his money into as many different investments as he could find. He had stocks, bond, managed futures, mutual funds, partnerships, and annuities. Every month an avalanche of monthly statements was in his mailbox.

Sandy started noticing a few months later that his usually organized files were starting to get difficult to maintain. There was so much paper. He pushed paper when he was an engineer, and it wasn't so much fun to push paper in retirement. He found he cared a lot less about any one investment, since any particular investment was such a small part of his total portfolio it didn't have much impact on his success. Sandy started to get careless. He didn't want to track his investments as often, so he didn't bother to update his monitoring work. His wife asked how the investment portfolio was performing, and he didn't really know for sure.

Tax time rolled around, and Sandy tried to pull together the papers for his accountant. To his frustration, he found that it was difficult to find all the proper documents. In some cases, he had to call brokers to get the information. In other cases, he had to back to confirmation slips to total his stock purchases. The accountant was ready to go, but

Sandy was delaying him. Finally, Sandy reached his frustration level, and decided that over time he would simplify his life and move his investments to something easier, such as CDs.

Let's analyze Sandy's action from several viewpoints. He did a lot of things well. He did his homework before making an investment. At first, he set a reasonable plan for monitoring. He communicated his concerns with the manager, and received and understood the manager's position. In the end, he was uncomfortable and fired the manager. *He forgot to design his investments around his comfort level.*

Diversify Your Portfolio

Diversification is an overused word in the investment industry. It is not, by itself, a single key to success. However, it definitely can help create peace of mind. Sandy had all his eggs in a carefully selected basket. With one investment to live and die with, he gave himself no stability. Either he had selected a good manager or he hadn't. The market would either go up or down.

Imagine Sandy's attitude toward the manager if that same stock account had been only 10 percent of Sandy's total portfolio. The monthly fluctuations would have been very easy to tolerate. Sandy might have stayed with the manager and enjoyed the next up market, vindicating his thorough investment search. *By varying the exposure to an investment, you affect the level of psychological pressure you put on yourself.* The less exposure, the more you can take an "I can live with it" attitude toward the investment. No single investment in a well-diversified portfolio will significantly impact the overall portfolio.

At first, Sandy did not diversify at all. This left him in the most vulnerable position. It's easy to see how an investor can get nervous and make emotional decisions when put in this position. Sandy was only human and responded to the pressure by adding more diversification.

I know an individual on the West Coast who became a real estate broker. He made a lot of money in sales commissions and was quite successful throughout the 1970s. He saw real estate going up and decided to invest in some deals himself, especially ones that he thought were exceptional. He put all his extra investment dollars into real estate, and at one point owned eight houses besides the one in which he lived. Then, along came some tax law changes and a recession, and he was in trouble. He had put all his eggs in one basket, and the basket began to come apart. His sales commissions fell dramatically. The value of real estate was on the decline. With great difficulty, he sold off the investment properties at slight losses, but could not come up with enough cash to pay the Internal Revenue Service. He had to negotiate with the government for extensions of time to pay his tax bill. Wouldn't it have been easier to diversify away from his industry or keep some of his money liquid so that it would be available in case of an emergency?

Diversification Can Be Overdone

If putting all your eggs in one basket is dangerous, what do you think about trying to buy a little of a lot of different investments? Diversification frequently becomes an excuse for buying too little of too many investments. The investor takes the attitude that he can afford to lose all of any single investment without hurting himself. This can become an excuse for becoming sloppy and not paying enough attention to a portfolio. It can also lead to an "I don't care" attitude. Without investments being properly monitored, the entire portfolio becomes a poorly performing collection of investment odds and ends.

Sandy overdid it at the end of the story. By getting into too many things he solved the problem of underdiversifying but created a problem with paperwork. He no longer cared what happened to any single investment, because each piece of his portfolio was such a small part of the total.

Overdiversifying can also lead to higher costs in managing your portfolio. Sometimes brokers and financial planners will suggest a diversified set of investments and break a portfolio down into many little pieces. You should know that some investments have discount transaction fees when purchased in larger quantity. The problem is that if you break your portfolio into enough pieces, each piece becomes small and no discounts are available. This produces the maximum commission to the selling agent. I am not saying here that all diversified portfolios are an attempt by your financial advisor to run up the cost of diversifying your portfolio. You should just know that there is a price to overdiversifying, just as there is danger in not diversifying enough.

Diversify to Your Balance point

Each investor will be different, but all investors have a point where investments are diversified to a comfort level without being overdiversified. Monitoring is made as easy as possible, and each investment, while being significant, is not an overwhelming percentage of the total portfolio. For most investors, a portfolio of three to five different, noncorrelated investments should reduce risk to a comfortable level without overdiversifying. With a balanced portfolio, it's much easier for the investor to stay mentally balanced. As we've already discussed, *the balanced mental state is one of considering more alternatives and logical decision making.*

Many professional traders have a saying that you have to get your investment position down to the point where you can sleep at night. I think this is excellent advice. You have better things to do with your life than spending it worrying about your investments. Diversify just to the point where your total portfolio is not burning a hole in your stomach lining and yet at the same time each investment is significant to you. Hopefully, you'll appreciate the peace of mind this strategy will give you.

How many stocks one should own.

What is my comfort level of risk, down 30% or any stock.

87

say 20K form ⟹ 70K investment only?

Chapter Thirteen —

How Is Everyone Compensated?

I have served as both an expert witness and an arbitrator in many securities and futures arbitration cases. Most of these cases focus on clients trying to get compensation for losses they believed were caused by poor or inappropriate advice given by a broker, financial planner, or advisor. Virtually all the client cases in which I've been involved include a selling agent who gives the client sales points that the investor thinks of as advice. The client realizes much later—much too late—that he or she was not given advice but was sold the investment. Let's follow the story of how Dr. Irving Cohen invested his hard-earned pension dollars.

Dr. Cohen was a successful facial/neck surgeon in a large midwestern city. He loved his work, and he was considered among the top in his specialty. A workaholic, he was able to make about $1 million per year. Cash flow was certainly not a problem.

Doctors are trained extensively in medicine, but not at all in investments. Dr. Cohen had the enviable problem of what to do with his large and rapidly growing pension plan. Just after medical school, Dr. Cohen had a bad experience with a broker-managed futures investment that went down, so that was not an alternative. He decided to buy a variety of quality mutual funds and hold them until retirement.

A broker with a respected Wall Street brokerage firm finally got through to the doctor, and, although he lived in a different city, insisted on an appointment. He wanted the chance to present his plan for the doctor's pension. The broker insisted that buying and holding a variety of mutual funds was not much of a plan for such a sizable amount of money. Dr. Cohen thought that there was a thread of logic to the broker's arguments, and agreed to meet with him the following week.

The broker's branch manager came along to the meeting, since they wanted to show Dr. Cohen that they were seriously interested in having him as their client. They indicated that they were major players in the institutional side of the stock market, and that they also did investment banking deals, some of which would be great investments for the pension. If they spotted some that looked especially good, they would alert Dr. Cohen to these deals for his pension. Dr. Cohen was impressed. They had gone to a lot of trouble to come 500 miles to see him, and the branch manager had taken the time to come along with the broker. Dr. Cohen started thinking that his pension was of the size where it could be considered institutional, and perhaps he should try out this new firm.

Things started out slowly. Several mutual funds were sold, and a portfolio was constructed out of the stocks that the brokerage office was following. In the first month, two sizable positions were bought and sold for a profit. Dr. Cohen thought that this was why institutions did better than the average investor. They could buy and sell in size and make profits in less than 30 days. The doctor moved all his remaining mutual funds to the broker, and more stocks were bought and sold. The doctor's portfolio was now turning over slightly faster than once per month. That meant that each month there was approximately the same dollars of buys and sells as there were dollars in Dr. Cohen's account.

A few positions got pretty large, approaching 25 percent of the portfolio. However, these tended to be held only a few weeks, so these big positions never stayed long enough to worry the doctor. With his medical practice demanding most of his attention, he let the brokers manage his account. When they suggested a new stock, he just went along with it and agreed to the purchase.

After about a year, including some positive and negative months, the brokers went into a large position of a regional pizza company, Pizza Pies Unlimited. The brokerage company was an investment banker in the stock, and counted Pizza Pies' president as one of its clients. The pizza company had expanded successfully and needed more capital. The brokers went out to raise the money. They put a sizable amount of the stock in the doctor's portfolio.

Suddenly, the bad news came out about the pizza company's financial strength. Bankruptcy loomed on the horizon. The brokerage firm, for a variety of reasons, was also headed toward bankruptcy, so the brokers called the doctor and convinced him to move to another large, well-respected brokerage firm. The doctor went along with the move. Finally, around tax time, his CPA mentioned that the large position showed a huge loss. The doctor looked a little more closely, and became alarmed. After consulting his family attorney, a securities attorney was retained. The brokers, their managers, and their firms were brought to arbitration.

Finally, the doctor found out the truth about what had been going on. He had been given the other side of trades being done in the broker's office by other brokers. When an investment banking client was selling his shares with one broker in the office, those shares were being bought by the doctor's account. Many trades had been done by the broker as market maker on a net basis, which had allowed the firm to not charge commissions. They had, instead, marked up the trades for a hefty trading profit for themselves. The branch manager who had come along with the broker for that initial meeting was in partnership with the broker on the account, and had received half the commissions generated by the doctor's account. In addition, the doctor discovered that his broker was having problems throughout the period with a cocaine habit, and the firm had been knowledgeable of the broker's condition.

At this point, Dr. Cohen was no longer naive. He now fully realized the game that had been played on him. An expert witness found that the account had been churned to generate commissions for the brokers. Dr. Cohen was able to recover some of his losses, but had to spend a pile of money on legal fees and a tremendous amount of precious time to reach a settlement.

Let's examine how the doctor could have changed the outcome.

How Is Everyone Compensated?

Investors should always understand how each individual is compensated in an investment deal. While this certainly doesn't guarantee that you can spot someone trying to jam something down your throat for a commission, it can at least help you understand where potential conflicts of interest exist and perhaps put you on guard to an advisor's motives.

For example, say you hire a registered investment advisor that only manages stocks and is paid a fee on the size of the portfolio. In a conversation about bonds, the manager expresses a very negative opinion about bonds as investment vehicles. By understanding that the advisor's compensation is tied to stocks, you can be cautious about the advice he is giving you about bonds.

If a broker is recommending a real estate partnership with 7 percent front-end commission for himself, 3 percent for his firm in general partner fees, and 5 percent commission for legal, accounting, and appraisal fees, then several questions might arise:

1. Is a less expensive alternative available?
2. Is this appropriate for me, or is the broker trying to sell this because his firm is pushing it?
3. How much of the broker's total compensation is tied to selling this deal or stock?
4. Can the commission or fee on a particular investment be negotiated down if I am a good client?

Remember, there are good and bad people in every profession. Sometimes it seems as though we only hear about the bad guys, since they always make the news. There are many diligent, trustworthy brokers/advisors. I have personally seen brokers do things for clients that decrease their own commissions. I have seen them provide some services for free, hoping to make it up on other investments. I *am not* saying that you should stop trusting your broker's advice; however, you should always be on your guard. I believe any reputable advisor or broker would prefer his or her clients to be knowledgeable investors and to ask tough questions. In the end, good advisors will prosper as they and their clients successfully grow together.

Chapter Fourteen —

Avoid
Information Overload

A lot of this book has been devoted to increasing your awareness about how you process information on investments. You now have many ways to avoid or minimize the frustration of investing your assets. At this point, my hope is that you have resolved to take control of your situation, learn more about investing, strive to improve your performance, and reduce your frustration. I would be pleased if I've motivated you to make some changes.

Many investors have a self-improvement attitude toward their investment decisions. They subscribe to all the financial newspapers, magazines, and newsletters. They start the day listening to a business news program, and end the day watching a recap of the day's business events. They attend seminars, talk to advisors, keep some indicators of their own, and become sponges for information on investing. Here's the story of one such individual.

Neal Johnson had been an accountant for 40 years. He had spent his life working with numbers, and was quite capable with both math and computers. As he approached retirement, he decided to prepare himself for managing his affairs, since he would now have the time. He started reading books, subscribed to a few newsletters, and attended seminars on managing retirement accounts. Upon his retirement date, he elected the lump-sum distribution from his retirement plan, and rolled the money over into an IRA-rollover to defer taxes on the distribution until he used the money later in life.

Mr. Johnson felt he was prepared to take over the day-to-day management of his investments. He knew all the terms, and started keeping a set of indicators that told him how his stocks were doing. He started a covered options writing program, which was designed to reduce the overall volatility of his portfolio. He enjoyed increasing his knowledge, and, therefore, continued to expand his indicators, go to seminars, and read books. A year of average performance disappointed him, but did not deter him from his quest to become a better investor.

A violent and significant drop in the market shocked both him and his wife. She had gone along with his plans so far, but this alarmed her, and she asked him to take a little less risk with their moneys. He decided to diversify the risk a little more. More indicators were added to his daily updates. He started looking around for more investments, and began to receive tons of information on alternate investments. Mr. Johnson was now making very few investment decisions. Actually, he found himself straining to make investment decisions, because he couldn't come to a clear-cut conclusion on what all the information he received was telling him to do. One indicator would tell him to buy a stock, while another would tell him to sell it. One broker liked mutual funds; the next broker discouraged investing in them. One advisor was a proponent of mutual fund timing, while a newsletter he subscribed to advised a buy-and-hold approach. What was he to do? He had spent inordinate amounts of time studying investments to the point where he was very knowledgeable of the language, theories, and vehicles of investing. He was in a mental state I call "analysis paralysis."

Finally, frustrated over the time he had wasted over the first few years of retirement, he decided to enjoy life a little more. He selected several different advisors, and diversified his portfolio among them so that the total was reasonably stabilized. He monitored the performance from time to time so that he didn't drive himself crazy with the day-to-day fluctuations. Once a quarter, he would have lunch with his advisors to update strategies and to stay in touch with what was important. He volunteered some of his time to a local charity, became active in local politics, and he and his wife started taking more trips to visit their children and grandchildren.

What can we learn from Neal Johnson? He eventually ended up with a very workable arrangement, but spent some frustrating years getting there. One would think that by having knowledge about investments, Neal would have a distinct advantage over the normal person in investing his moneys. Unfortunately, he seemed to have more difficulty because of the increased knowledge.

When analyzing an investment, one indicator says buy while another says sell. One advisor says he's bullish; another says she's bearish. Each newsletter has a different formula for making a person wealthy beyond his or her wildest dreams. Investors want to do something, but with so many opinions out there, who or what should they believe? Every investment worries them, because they know about and dwell on the risks. They are stressed because they don't have all the information they need. If they could only lay their hands on the right newsletter or read the right book, they could finally be successful investors.

Just the Facts, Please

When investors seek opinions from a wide variety of sources, they frequently are searching for a consensus. Presumably, if many opinions point to a single answer, then that must be the way to go. But the markets don't work that way. Every time someone buys, someone else is selling, and both investors believe that they are making the right move. More often than not, however, consensus information is incorrect information and signals a market move in the opposite direction.

Investors would be better served to form their own opinion. They must separate other people's opinions and the facts they present. If an advisor says, "The market will go higher," that is his opinion. If the market is at an all-time high, that is a fact. When I am interviewed by someone for publication, one of the last questions that I'm frequently asked is, "Where is the market going?" Should the investor care where I think the market is going? Each day, the smart investor must deal with the market as it is that day. If the market is going against him, he must guard against risk and frustration. If the market is going his way, he must guard against overoptimism or taking profits too soon. Wishing and hoping the market does something will not make it happen.

If you want to know other people's opinions, then when you hear an opinion, flag what you hear in your brain as an opinion, not a fact. If you see me or anyone else quoted as saying the market is going up or down, repeat to yourself, "That's his opinion; I'll form my own." This will help you take responsibility for your own decisions, and will help you gather facts to support your own opinion.

Collect Enough Information
to Make the Decision

When you form your own opinion, you need to gather facts and information. No matter how hard you try, you will never be able to gather all the information on an investment. However, this can become a crutch for never making an investment decision. You think, "I'm not sure, so I'll just see what my broker thinks." When he disagrees with you, you ask your brother, an accountant, who says, "You'll end up paying too much tax with that strategy." You can keep doing this forever, but you'll never get the final, perfect opinion or all the facts about the investment.

If you want to get other people's opinions on an investment strategy, you should find out what would cause them to change their opinion. In other words, if an expert on the gold market tells you gold is going up, ask him what would cause him to change his mind. All too often, investors hear other people's opinions that convince them to get into an investment. However, they don't have a clue about how to get out of the investment.

You should also realize that when people ask the opinions of others, they tend to be looking for other opinions that justify their own thinking. Most investors who ask an "expert's" opinion simply are hoping the expert agrees with them. It would actually be more useful to hear opinions opposite one's own in order to open the mind to alternatives. However, it is very difficult for the normal person to have the courage to follow his or her own analysis when it comes to a different conclusion. Yet following the crowd is usually the worst thing to do. By the time most investors agree on something, the move has already happened, and it's too late to jump in.

It does not take forever to get enough information to form your own opinion. Pull together whatever you can in a reasonable time period and at a reasonable cost. At that point, take your best shot at a decision. Realize that you do not have perfect knowledge, and never will. Dwelling on this fact or worrying about it won't accomplish anything. Simply move on to forming an opinion, then execute your investment decision.

Chapter Fifteen

Make a Decision, Then Act!

When a financial advisor gives advice to a client, there is always a trade-off between trying to educate the client about numerous suitable investments and narrowing down the list for the client to one or two recommendations. Picking the final choice of an investment for a client is always the easiest way. It allows the advisor to select his or her favorite, and the client doesn't have to work so hard thinking or taking responsibility for making a decision.

But, as in many things in life, the easy way may not produce the best results. It is important for investors to know their alternatives and take responsibility for making sure the final choice is the one for them. The problem is that when an advisor presents to an investor all the possible investment alternatives, the investor frequently goes into a state of mental inaction. Let's examine the case of a couple as they approach retirement.

Mr. and Mrs. Whittington had lived the good life. He was a top-level executive of a Fortune 500 company, and before she retired his wife had been a successful professional. They had reared two kids. Both were active in tennis and golf. A large part of their retirement benefits had been accumulated in Mr. Whittington's corporate pension plan, but they had also put away a little in private savings.

Their daughter eventually became a broker and worked on a bond trading desk at a major brokerage firm. Although she didn't specialize in a variety of investments, she had enough knowledge to keep her mom and dad out of major trouble. Their private investments had appreciated and the corporate pension had increased modestly. Clearly, they were in good shape as they approached their retirement years.

Then, without a lot of warning, Mr. Whittington's company went through some downsizing. Unfortunately, Mr. Whittington's job was among those eliminated. He was three years from retirement, but financial times were tough for the company and they were forced to make some difficult decisions to compete globally. There were no hard feelings between the Whittingtons and the company. They were left with a decent severance, his pension benefits, and their private savings that had been invested with their daughter's advice in a few good stocks and mutual funds.

The plan was for Mr. Whittington to find a job that might run for three to five years. At that point, they would both be retired and would live off their investments, travel, and play more golf and tennis. He attacked the job market with a vengeance, only to discover that a position for someone who had enjoyed his high level in the corporate world was difficult to find. They lived off of their investment portfolio, which was not large enough to cover their cost of living. Mrs. Whittington, tired of seeing the savings under such pressure, decided to go back to work in her profession as a contract employee. They could make ends meet, but were unable to build their financial strength for the future. Uncertainty ruled their lives for the moment.

Meanwhile, they both became increasingly worried about their investments. Their portfolio had been put together over many years. Many of the investments were growth-oriented and had been purchased when Mr. Whittington had been bringing home a sizable income. They provided some income, but not enough to meet their retirement needs. The stock market had continued to make new highs, but the Whittingtons worried that if a severe recession hit they might not have income streams at the same time that their portfolio might decrease substantially.

They met with their daughter as well as a number of other financial advisors, and all of them said the same thing. They were not managing their investments. They were simply holding them. Other people made the decisions about Mr. Whittington's pension plan and other people had made the decisions to buy the mutual funds and stocks. The little responsibility that the Whittingtons had taken had been easy to take with a large salary coming in each month. But now the investment decisions meant the difference between working a lot more years and retiring comfortably. When the pressure was turned up a notch, indecision set in. They were looking for the magic answer to all their problems.

Finally, Mr. Whittington decided to go back into the insurance business. He had been an agent early in his career and decided that being self-employed was the only way that he could expect to earn a living at this point in his life. Mrs. Whittington continued to work on a contract basis, and all plans to retire were put off into the future. The portfolio remained unchanged and they continued to worry about the condition of the market.

Let's look at how the mental decision-making process led them to their current condition. All their investments had come with information and logical reasons to buy them at the time. Strong recommendations had made the decisions to purchase simple to make. Now, with the pressure of relying on the portfolio, decisions became harder to make.

Make Decisions without the Pressure

The Whittingtons' situation reminds me of a professional golfer on the last day of the U.S. Open who needs to make a five-foot putt to clinch the victory by one stroke. He's so close to having it made. He's practiced all his life. He's played in lesser tournaments and won. He's been successful by most standards, but he knows that winning the U.S. Open will take his career to another level in prestige and endorsements. His nerves make it almost impossible for him to function normally.

There are three ways he can approach the situation. The worst would be to mentally dwell on what would happen if he missed the putt, went to a playoff, and lost the tournament. Everyone would say he choked and couldn't win the big one. If he spends long enough dwelling on the negative possibilities, he will be so nervous, he will surely miss it.

Another approach he might take is to fill his mind with positive thoughts of what might happen if he sinks the putt and becomes the reigning champion of the U.S. Open with all the trappings and prestige that the victory would bring. He could imagine the cheering crowds and the television interviews with the newest hero of the golfing world. This would tend to excite him. Quite possibly a simple five-foot putt would go flying by the hole recklessly. He might leave the ball farther away than it was in the case of the first putt and put himself in a position to not share in the lead at all.

Both these possible approaches would put the golfer in an emotionally charged state, complete with nerves and plenty of adrenaline. The golfer's thoughts are focused on one scenario to the exclusion of the other. A third and perhaps healthier attitude to take toward the putt is to treat it like every other putt. The golfer might realize that if the putt is missed, he would like to leave it close to the hole so that he can tie for the lead. The golfer should stick to his routine, checking the environment, lining up the target line, and stroking smoothly through the ball. This way, he gives his mind the maximum chance of being in balance. He is concentrating on the things that make him a successful golfer and is mentally letting go of the results. This type of balance gives him the best chance for success in the long run. A "seasoned veteran" has been in this position many times and can stay focused on the routine. The rookie is the one who gets too emotionally high or low.

Investors put a lot of pressure on themselves. They worry about where the market is going, how much they will make, whether they are putting enough into an investment, or which investment they should choose. But add to that the fact that returns on the investment portfolio are critical to achieving some goal, and the pressure sometimes causes indecision. Just like the golfer, the investor should stick to the things that got him or her there. Get into some healthy habits with your investing, and continue those habits even when under more pressure. This will help you do the right thing and let the results take care of themselves.

Gather the Facts

One of the easiest tasks to do is to gather the facts. I've already explained how that can be done and how that can be overdone. Research the investment or idea as thoroughly as is reasonable for you, but set a time limit for yourself. You are not going to be an expert on every area of investment, but you can spot things you like and things that would concern you. Keep your eyes open for positive and negative points on a particular investment or investment strategy. You will never be able to gather all the facts about a situation. You need only the important facts to move on to a decision.

Just the Key facts !!

Make a Decision

The next step is more difficult, but certainly not impossible. In a balanced state of mind, without a lot of worrying about what future results might be, simply analyze the positives and negatives and take your best shot. If it looks okay, do it. If it doesn't, move on to other things. Remember, not making a decision is really a decision to do nothing. Make sure that you really want to make a decision to do nothing and that you're not ending up there by default or laziness.

Just Pull the Trigger

With facts in hand and a decision made, you might think that you are done. But the hardest thing to do is ahead. You now have to take action. Believe it or not, this is where all sorts of self-doubt and second-guessing enter the picture.

Say you decide to say yes to investment. You then call a broker and he says, "I'm not sure I like that investment." You might have decided to go ahead with a tax-advantaged investment, but at a family gathering your sister, a CPA, mentions, "I'd never do any tax-advantaged investments. All I've ever seen is problems with them." The thought of "Maybe I made the wrong decision" starts creeping in, introducing doubt into your mind. You start thinking about gathering more facts and you are back to the beginning again. You certainly are not ready to act decisively.

My way of acting decisively is based on something I learned many years ago. I went to engineering school in the early 1970s during the

Vietnam era. Since I was of draft age, I thought I'd hedge my chances. I figured if I were drafted, at least I could go as an officer if I signed up for Reserve Officers Training Corp. (ROTC). Part of the two-year curriculum was practice on the rifle range and education about shooting a weapon. I ended up qualifying as an expert marksman.

I learned that the key to successfully hitting the target is to simply pull the trigger without thinking when it seemed appropriate to do so. For those who have never shot a weapon, your body cannot remain perfectly motionless. Even your heart pumping and the blood flow moving through your body will cause some slight movement in your aim. So, as you look down the sights, the target will seem to move. When the target and sights line up for a fraction of a second, there is no time to think, "Did I do everything right? Should I wait for the next chance?" You've prepared yourself to make a good shot, so turn off your brain and pull the trigger, without any thought about the consequences of the shot. More often than not, you hit the target precisely where you wanted.

Shooting has a lot of analogies to investing. Just like the shooter getting ready to shoot, the investor must gather the facts. Next, the shooter takes aim, deciding to take a shot. The investor makes a decision concerning his or her portfolio. Finally, without thought, the shooter squeezes off the round, while the investor makes a call, writes a letter, or cuts a check. So the next time you seem to be having difficulty making a decision, think of the shooter and just pull the trigger.

Zen : let the arrow shoots itself !

Chapter Sixteen

Staying the Course—
The Toughest Decision

We have mostly been looking at the mistakes that investors make when they take avoidable risks, allow themselves to get greedy, or, by taking no action, put themselves in harm's way. But at the risk of confusing you, I would suggest that making a decision to be patient and simply let the investment make a return for you is one of the toughest investment decisions you'll ever make. Let's look at how Andy Murray, a mover and shaker of the business world, handles his investments.

Andy lived on the West Coast with his wife of 20 years. He was the supreme example of the decisive businessman. If you asked him for a decision on anything, he gathered whatever facts he could in the necessary time, formed an opinion on his best decision, and acted, accepting full responsibility for the decision. His philosophy was that he always gave it his best shot and that's all anyone could ever ask of him. It had served him well over his business career, as his company promoted him over and over again to positions of ever-increasing responsibility.

Andy and his wife were approaching middle age and the kids were off to college. They realized that retirement loomed in the distance as the next major step of their lives. Andy had been so comfortable in his ability to provide for his family from his successful business career, that investing had never seemed like a very important thing to spend much time on. He concentrated on making bigger and bigger pay checks and was a success by most people's standards.

However, they had become accustomed to the lifestyle that a successful corporate executive's salary could provide and hadn't put away nearly enough to retire in the same style they now lived. "No problem," he thought. "I'll just get an investment program going and with the kids gone, I'll be able to sock it away." Andy the expert decision maker set off to talk to financial planners, brokers, and money managers to gather some information and get a plan underway. He also decided to start setting aside some time each weekend to catch up on the financial news of the week, so that he might become more familiar with the various markets.

As usual, Mr. Decision had no trouble moving ahead. After a number of meetings with some financial experts, he decided to have investments managed by a financial planner near his office. He would be able to meet periodically with the advisor and felt comfortable with her approach to diversification and the management of risk. She had proposed a simple-to-understand dollar-cost averaging program in mutual funds. In this program Andy would invest a set amount of dollars in a diversified set of mutual funds each month. If a fund's price was higher, he would buy fewer shares of the fund; if the fund was down, he would buy more shares of the fund. He decided to put away 25 percent of his salary each month. His wife was in agreement, and their action plan was initiated.

Six months later, Andy decided it was time for an interim review. His advisor, Candice Murphy, explained that everything was on track. The conservative mutual funds they had selected had made some money for the first four months, then started pulling back. The dollar-cost averaging program was buying into the funds on the pullback. When they had another run up, he would own even more shares and should be pleased with the results. Andy's own reading of the market was that the market was heading down. He wasn't sure whether it was a short pullback or a big bear waiting to beat up his mutual funds, but watching the funds drift lower and throwing new money into losing positions at the time didn't seem sensible. So he informed Candice he would be staying with his current investments, but was going to build up some cash in a money market for a while and not buy any more mutual funds. She tried to remind him of their decision to dollar-cost average their mutual fund purchases. If he didn't buy the additional shares when the prices were down, then he would not own them as they went up during the next up market. But Andy had made his decision and was moving ahead with his plan.

The market reversed within the month. Andy was tied up with some trips overseas and three months later decided to get some updates on the funds. They were doing better now and were actually making new highs. The financial press was becoming fairly optimistic about the prospects for the market over the next year. Andy gave his planner a call and told her that he decided to invest his savings into the mutual funds. Another slightly more aggressive fund was added to the list to further diversify the portfolio.

About six months later, Andy read an article summarizing the past year in the markets and thought it would be good to review his portfolio against the article's market summary. The market had closed up 2 percent for the previous 12 months. He thought that surely he had done better than that since he owned professionally selected funds and had added to his positions. Much to his amazement, his planner reported that his time-weighted return, which measured his true return on all his dollars corrected for how long they had been invested, was down 2 percent. Andy was a bottom-line type of guy. He had been used to making decisions and getting results in the business world. He was used to cutting his losses short and moving forward. He informed the planner that he was going to find someone else to manage his assets who could get results.

This general story repeated itself a number of times, with Andy investing in well laid out plans. He would invest his money when he believed the timing was right. Then, after a period of time, he would become dissatisfied with the lack of progress and move on to something new. After some years, Andy was convinced the investing world was filled with a "bunch of idiots and incompetent managers!"

Sometimes You Have to Change Course. . . .

Andy's business success was due to his ability to make decisions. People who spend their lives waiting for something to happen will usually be waiting a long time. As I've pointed out in previous chapters, taking responsibility, gathering a reasonable amount of facts, considering the risks, and acting is a very appropriate way of approaching the world of investing. If something needs to be changed, then change it. It is also appropriate to achieve some business success. Andy had that talent and used it.

And Sometimes It's Better to Stay the Course

Sailors have a term that describes moving straight ahead. They frequently find themselves with the wind in their sails and the boat slicing through the water. The term "stay the course" means to do nothing and let what you've already done continue to do its job for you. No major change in strategy is necessary because what you have already done is working fine.

When Andy went to his first six-month review, he had a dollar-cost averaging program that was doing exactly what it was designed to do. He was buying more shares in the down market and accumulating a bigger position for the next move up. Staying the course would have meant continuing to buy the shares as the market went lower. However, Andy didn't feel comfortable doing that. He changed course in midstream and held back his savings. He then invested the extra money at a higher price, increasing, rather than decreasing, his average price. The timing of the investments caused the loss, not the selection of the funds. Firing his financial planner was like shooting the messenger that brings bad news. It solved nothing.

The Right Thing to Do May Be to Stay with Your Current Approach

In writing this book, I've given you a lot of actions or things to consider in future investing endeavors. Here, I'd like to give you the opposite. Many times in successful investing, you sit and wait for opportunities. Other times, you sit and wait for your investments to appreciate. Still other times you have to patiently wait for an investing strategy to make it through a rough period and become strong again.

In *Reminiscences of a Stock Operator,* a thinly disguised biography of the famous stock speculator Jesse Livermore, he offers some timeless advice: "And right here let me say one thing: After spending many years in Wall Street and after making and losing millions of dollars I want to tell you this: *It never was my thinking that made the big money for me. It was always my sitting. Got that? My sitting tight! It is not a trick to all be right on the market. You always find lots of early bulls in bull markets and early bears in bear markets.* . . . Men who can both be right and sit tight are uncommon. I found it one of the hardest things to learn. . . . That is why so many men in Wall Street, who are not at all in the sucker class, . . . nevertheless lose money. The market does not beat them. They beat themselves, because though they have brains, *they cannot sit tight.*"

I believe that patience should be on the long list of requirements for good investing. As mentioned above, it is most assuredly one of the most difficult things for an investor to master. Next time you are making a decision, simply add one additional choice: "Am I patient and sticking to my current investment plan?"

patience
sit ———— (after setting stop loss ?)
unless you have a definitely better
choice , don't move !!

e.g. move out of Altice
move out of SAP into Chipcom ...
move out of 3Com ?!

Chapter Seventeen ——

To Succeed, Lose the Ego

We human beings let our egos get in the way of so many good things. How many disputes are caused by stubborn egos? How many divorces are caused by two people who, because of egos, won't allow themselves to see the other person's point of view? Mergers are frequently held up because of how the subsequent company's organization will affect the major egos of the board members or the chief executive officers. Politicians frequently make decisions based on their egos rather than the will of the people. Let's look at the story of an investor with a major ego.

Dr. Richard Laner was Mr. Important at a major St. Louis regional hospital. His whole career was storybook material. Reared in a wealthy west St. Louis suburb, he attended a prominent private prep school. He completed his undergraduate and medical school education at famous eastern ivy league schools. He was the best in all his classes and was highly recruited out of medical school. He decided to return home to St. Louis. He felt like the conquering knight, home from the wars to garner the respect and admiration of those who had known him from childhood.

A few years into his career as a cardiologist, he was named the head of the cardiology department—the youngest person to ever hold that position at this institution. Surgeons, nurses, and administrators were at his disposal. He was treated as royalty and he rather liked it. After all, he was one of the best in his profession in the country. He was making big money. He had his college debts paid off, and he could start building a significant investment portfolio to set himself up for early, luxurious retirement.

Dr. Laner's first attempt at investing was quite simple. When returning to St. Louis, he simply opened accounts at the same bank his family had been using for the past 50 years. Extra money, not needed for the bills, went into money market accounts or CDs. He was immediately assigned a private banker, who would take care of his banking needs in a flash. Eventually, he had over $100,000 in various CDs, and he decided to start a real investing program. After all, CDs were for smaller investors. He now had a significant amount and more would be added regularly. At his present pace, within a few years, he would be controlling millions of dollars in personal and pension moneys.

His private banker decided the best place to start would be their trust department. Their portfolio managers had an average of 30 years of experience and had known his father. They presented a strategy of stocks and bonds that would conservatively grow his portfolio. He was impressed with the service and the respect the bank had given him so far, so he agreed to the plan.

In the next two years, Dr. Laner had input approximately $600,000, and his portfolio was worth $614,000. He wasn't impressed with the results. He should be getting better returns. He started feeling that maybe he hadn't been assigned the best portfolio manager at the bank and voiced his complaints to the private banker. She quickly passed the word to the trust department and their most senior portfolio manager was assigned to Dr. Laner's account. Another year and a half later, they produced only slightly better results. The doctor decided he would move on to someone who could appreciate his account and get him the results he deserved.

A very old, respected investment banking house was located in St. Louis and Dr. Laner met one of the principals over drinks at the country club. He told the doctor that typically trust departments are very conservative, sometimes to the point of boring. He deserved someone who could look out for his interests, get him in on significant deals, and be a little more entrepreneurial. The doctor, after being disappointed with his first endeavors in investing, told the investment broker he just wanted a good bottom line. The broker didn't have a problem with that and asked the doctor to let him show what he could do. Dr. Laner thought he was finally going to get first-class service on his portfolio and moved his account to the broker's house.

A blend of conservative, dividend-paying stocks and newly issued securities were moved into his portfolio. Some went up. Some went down. Buys were issued. Sales were made. There certainly was a lot more activity. The doctor figured someone now was finally taking care of his account. They met occasionally at the club and talked investments. The broker had an engaging personality and could tell some great stories. He knew something about every stock in the portfolio and related where the potential was in every position. Dr. Laner knew he had finally found his investment pro and felt totally comfortable with his new financial advisor.

A few years passed and the market for newly issued securities had a few rough years in a row. Dr. Laner's CPA, from a prominent "big six" accounting firm, started asking questions about some losses the doctor was claiming on his taxes. Dr. Laner didn't have any good answers because his broker was always so upbeat about the prospects for his portfolio. After some quick research, he discovered that, despite some exceptional winners, the overall portfolio had not kept pace with the general market.

Dr. Laner felt somewhat betrayed. He deserved better than this shabby treatment. His large and ever-growing portfolio should have had the best advice. Everyone he worked with or hired as advisors seemed to make mistakes with his portfolio. He couldn't make mistakes in his profession or people died. Why couldn't he find someone who could get the job done right?

He finally decided that "if you want something done right, you should do it yourself." He was a pretty smart guy and it shouldn't be too difficult to keep tabs on a few stocks. He started out by subscribing to a few newsletters and moving his brokerage account to a large discount house to save on the commissions. They didn't offer any advice, but that was fine with him since he was going to make all his own decisions.

He found several stocks that seemed to be run by individuals like himself with impressive credentials. They came from solid families with connections. He started investing in these stocks. Depending on how good he felt about it, he bought more or less in each position. He didn't like having to waste his precious time on his investments, but he felt he had to if he expected to get good bottom-line results.

A year or so later, he noticed one of the stocks slipping badly. He picked up the phone and called the company. After he had informed them who he was, he was told by the president's secretary that he should talk to shareholder relations. The doctor felt that an important investor like himself should talk to "the top guy." The secretary apologized politely, but emphatically told the doctor that there were just too many calls for the president to handle and that the shareholder relations department was his only choice. He grumbled, but accepted. The shareholder relations person was polite and informative, but did not leave Dr. Laner with a sufficient comfort level, so he made a quick call to his broker and sold the position for a loss.

The general market was heading into one of its normal, periodic slumps and was off 15 percent. Most of the stocks in Dr. Laner's portfolio were now unrealized losses. Another stock hit the skids. Dr. Laner called the company to find out what was going on only to get a recording saying that the company was going into reorganization. Until details were worked out, no phone number was available. Dr. Laner became concerned and almost immobilized by the decline in the value of his portfolio. He had never failed at anything before so miserably and couldn't figure out why he shouldn't be able to figure out how to make money in the markets. He became one more frustrated investor.

Service Doesn't Equal Return on Investment

Dr. Laner was searching for good service as an indication to his ego that he would receive good results. Great service may be flattering and I like service as much as the next guy, but service and performance are two very different things. A number of brokerage firms, money management firms, and trust departments have provided great service, raised a lot of money, and delivered mediocre results.

I am not saying that service should be ignored. If a client is not comfortable with the level of service a financial advisor delivers, the client leaves and goes elsewhere. If service is at an acceptable level, concentrate on the investment's rewards and risks.

Egos Are Dangerous to Have When Investing

Dr. Laner was a person with a huge ego. He was sure of himself, and people around him treated him like royalty. Everything he did seemed to work out well. Many might mistake Dr. Laner's attitude as self-confident, but there's a big difference between self-confidence and a big ego. Most people with large egos have poor self-confidence and seem to be trying to use their egos to hide their lack of self-confidence. The more self-confidence you have, the less you need to satisfy your ego.

The markets seem to frustrate investors with large egos, because they think of themselves as smarter, bigger, or more in tune with the market. In reality, they are not. The market can then proceed to shred their egos by repeatedly treating them to lesson after lesson on how not to invest.

The market is like a potentially dangerous but useful tool. A power drill in the hands of an experienced woodcrafter can work all sorts of magic. The same tool in the hands of a young child can do serious injury to the child. But, should the woodcrafter ever let his ego get in the way of safety and become sloppy or careless, the tool can remind him of how dangerous it really is.

You should not fear the market. But you need to recognize that you'll never completely master it. Simply respect it, and keep your ego out of the investing process. This will keep you from a great deal of frustration, and help you succeed as an investor.

Chapter Eighteen ———

——— The Markets Are Not Random, and Other Personal Thoughts

Many learned people have proposed that markets are random and that you can't beat some passive approach when taking into account the costs of trading. Most individuals expressing these random market theories simply talk about or teach investing. On the other hand, a number of my friends in the investing community and myself have been managing money with some success for many years. It is totally illogical to me that anyone could think that markets are random.

A market is nothing more than a place where buyer and seller come together. Both put their money on the line. Both believe they are making a decision in their best interest. If either party to a trade doesn't like what he or she is getting, no trade occurs. When an imbalance exists in normal supply and demand, then prices move to bring supply and demand into balance. (There's that "balance" word again. I use the "B" word a lot—have you noticed?) In other words, say there are a lot of investors that believe a company is about to be taken over at a higher price. The demand for the stock will typically be more than the selling pressure. Prices will then rise to a level where the buying and selling demand is in equilibrium. On the other hand, say everyone panicked and thought that the market was crashing. Then there would be more selling pressure than buying pressure. Prices would drop to a point where some buyer finally thought the value was good enough to take a risk on buying. Again, the prices would move to create equilibrium between the buyers and sellers.

If everyone who invested in the markets had random minds, then I would agree that the markets would be random. I prefer to believe that most investors have an approach to investing, and that their approach doesn't change every other day. Their approach may be sound, or it may be totally unsound, but their final decisions will definitely influence the markets. Therefore, there has to be a nonrandom behavior to the markets, because the human minds that move the money in or out of the markets are not random. Presumably, if we could know what each investor in a stock was going to do at any point in time, we could accurately predict the supply and demand forces. We would then have an accurate indication of future price movements. It's absurd to think of this as random behavior.

Your Personal Life Affects Your Investment Results

Most investors would probably give very little thought to how their noninvesting life affects their investment performance and frustrations. When you think about it, there is no way your personal life can remain separate from your investments, because the sum of your investing and noninvesting lives equals your total life. Time and mental effort given to investments cannot be allotted to noninvestment activities.

The busy, overworked executive who receives a call from a broker doesn't have the time to think about an investment, so she says, "Sounds good to me." A struggling young investor hopes to make a killing to get him out of his perceived mediocre life. A potential divorce causes another investor to be more conservative than he should, since he might be using the portfolio to settle with his spouse. An individual who had a little too much to drink last night doesn't feel like tackling that dry, legal prospectus and paperwork because of a dull headache. A desk jockey is tired after a long day at the office, and decides to put off reading that sales brochure that he requested from his broker. A salesperson, who's had a few too many coffees and sodas with caffeine, finds herself unable to focus with an unemotional state of mind. Instead of making clear decisions, she becomes emotional about lack of results and vows to fire her financial advisor.

If you want to improve your performance at something, ask yourself one simple question: *"What do I have to do to be the best I can be at this?"* An Olympic athlete spends his life focusing on one event. His goal is very focused. He works on his body and mind to meld them together to achieve a gold medal performance. His whole life is balanced around being the best he can be. If his personal life cannot handle the strain of focused training and intrudes on the training, he is not going to perform as well. The news reports are full of athletes who underperform when contract disputes, personal tragedies, or organizational changes intrude on playing the sport. Home games are probably easier than away games because athletes can organize their day in a normal fashion and maintain a better focus on the game. When out of town, schedules are varied, and it is harder for the body and mind to keep the same successful rhythm.

Personal stress definitely affects your investments. I have witnessed numerous clients living with the stress of failing businesses. In most cases, they become excessively nervous about their investments. They know that their portfolios are the only buffer they have between their current status and bankruptcy. They monitor the investments too closely, become overly emotional, and generally, become very poor investors. Other forms of personal stress can be caused by getting married, having a child, getting a divorce, losing a job, retiring, or losing a spouse. Be aware that personal stress will affect your ability to be a successful, balanced investor.

I am not proposing that you change your whole life just to become a better investor. *However, you should consider how your personal life affects your investing successes and/or failures.* Many years ago I would make more impulsive decisions after drinking several cups of coffee. The caffeine apparently was speeding up my brain and decreasing my ability to focus and make logical decisions. I stopped consuming caffeine, and found it much easier to make investment decisions. In addition, I became more relaxed and less stressed in other areas of my life.

Do you give yourself the tools, time, and training you need to become a better investor or client? Are there some areas you could work on in your personal life that could reduce your personal stress and improve your ability to focus, thereby improving how you invest? Give it some thought.

Reducing Costs versus Increasing Returns

I am familiar with quite a few people who come from families of modest financial means. I count myself among them. A frequent comment on investing from people trying to make ends meet is "I can't seem to save enough to ever have an investment portfolio." They always seem to be trying to get to the next paycheck. Major financial expenditures like autos and college expenses are dealt with a "we'll cross that bridge when we get to it" attitude.

Saving money in life is an interesting problem in itself. Almost anyone committed to putting away a few dollars per month could do it. Some people make a game out of clipping coupons or have fun negotiating with a retail clerk to get a good deal. Using their time and mental effort, they reduce their costs of living the same lifestyle. If they are committed, a small savings can be accumulated. With enough savings, this becomes a potential investing portfolio.

Unfortunately, some people spend too much time and energy on reducing costs and trying to save money, and that can get in the way of investing. To that, your response might be an outraged, "Are you out of your mind? What about saving on brokerage commissions or negotiating a better real estate deal on your house?" I would agree that these parts of the investing process are oriented toward reducing costs, but focusing on just reducing costs, and not on the returns and risk, can lead you astray.

For example, say you spend a great deal of time reading the sale ads in the newspaper. Then you might run around to four or five stores to get the best deals. The total savings you might amass might not be equal to the cost of gas for your car and the time you spent obtaining the best deals. On the other hand, you could spend that extra time and effort on your investment portfolio. You might learn of a new area that looks promising. You might be able to spend more time monitoring the results of your portfolio or considering changes to be made. You might take the time to read that dry prospectus that might prevent you from making a big mistake. You might attend a one-hour seminar to learn more about tax rules or investment techniques. In about three hours, you could read this book!

Now let's look at what is to be gained from reducing costs versus increasing returns. The saver is reducing costs. He starts with whatever the cost would normally be and expends time and energy reducing the amount he pays for the same item or service. How low can he make costs go? Certainly he cannot get them to zero. Maybe down 5, 10, or even 15 percent? This might be worth some decent value. However, *there clearly is a limit to how much money an individual can save each year by reducing costs.*

On the other hand, consider the efforts of the investor. He spends his time and mental effort improving the results of his investments. What is his incentive? What is to be gained from concentrating on investments? Depending on the size of your portfolio, anything from a few dollars to millions. *There is no limit to the amount of theoretical gain that can be had if you spent your efforts on increasing your returns.*

Time is the one thing that we all have that has a finite limit. *If there is no limit to how much the investor can make, but a definite limit to the amount a person can save, the investor must spend his time attempting to increase returns in order to prosper.* The key is that without a portfolio to invest, this is only a dream. The larger the portfolio, the more important is your need to spend your time increasing your portfolio versus saving some costs. As in so many other areas, balance is so important. When your portfolio is small or nonexistent, saving money is the only thing you can do. When your portfolio reaches a larger amount, less emphasis should be put on reducing costs and more emphasis should be placed on increasing investment returns. As you progress through life and through various sizes of investments, a shift to concentrating on investing should happen smoothly. This requires a change in your behavior. Think about the energy and time you split between reducing costs and increasing investments. You need to decide whether or not you've struck the appropriate balance. I'm not saying that you shouldn't be prudent or economical. I am saying that you should have some balance in the time and mental effort spent between saving and investing.

Concentrate on the Process, and Let the Results Take Care of Themselves

We spend much of life worrying about outcomes. We worry about the kid down the block when we're little. We worry about that big exam, or the next ball game, or the first date, or the next promotion. If you take the time to think about it, you'd realize that worrying about the results does very little to successfully affect the final outcome. Actually, it may make you tense and cause you to perform at less than peak level.

If you insist on worrying about something, at least limit it to constructive worry. There are stressful events that you can do nothing about. There are other outcomes that, through your abilities or resources, you can change. If you are going to worry, concentrate on the latter rather than the former. *Focusing on the things you can change helps put you in control of your life.* Worrying about the outcome of an activity does little to improve your results. Indeed, it probably just helps eat a hole in your stomach lining.

Since I am an avid golfer, permit me to include an example of this concept using my favorite game. Say you have a 150-yard shot over water and sand bunkers to a small green with three tiers surrounded by deep rough with a cliff on the back side of the putting surface. If the golfer starts thinking through all the ways he can mess up the shot, he will become more nervous and probably have little chance of hitting a good shot. On the other hand, if the golfer focuses on hitting a simple, reasonably straight 150-yard shot, the ball will probably land on the green. He can then finish the hole and move on to the next hole. In golf, as in life, the more relaxed you are, the easier it seems to be to perform well. Focus on the swing, which you can do something about, rather than worrying about the negative things that might happen.

In a stock market example, you might focus on where your stop loss should be to control your risk rather than being concerned about which direction the market is going to move. The market will move whichever way it chooses, with or without your worrying about it. You are quite powerless to do anything about it. Why not focus on those things you can change? In a managed futures program, you might concentrate on how much risk money of your total assets you will allocate, rather than getting excited over how much you are winning or losing each day. In retirement, you might focus on the allocation of your investments with an objective of preserving principal and purchasing power.

Focusing on things you can control will help you achieve greater success with a lot less stress.

[handwritten: Control over ① plan ② diversification ③ balance of lives.]

Investing Is Like a Mirror

Investing is a mirror of life. Your abilities, stresses, and weaknesses all will be mirrored in your investments. Investors who are gamblers will tend to like fast-moving, high-risk investments. People who have a hard time making a decision will wait too long to buy something, then own it forever. Personal stress will affect performance. The mirror doesn't lie. Take some time to look into your mirror and understand yourself. It can only help your ability to invest wisely.

Lose Your Ego When Investing

Remember that the markets do not respect you or your ego. I have seen numerous smart, successful, egotistical investors get their egos shredded. If you have too much ego involved in your investing, or in your life for that matter, you'll just be more frustrated.

A friend remembered something I once said in an article that he thought summed it up well. He had the saying artistically scripted and framed and I have it on my wall as a daily reminder. It says "Unless you are humble in the face of the market, the market will see to it that you are humbled." Keep in mind that the market will fool most investors. The moment you think you have it all figured out is the precise moment the market will typically treat you to another lesson in humility.

[handwritten: It's not figured out. Form Hypothesis, test it, be a pig when you are right!]

Final Thoughts

I hope this book has given you many useful, practical thoughts on the process of good investing. It's up to you to take these general thoughts and make them specific to your situation. The easiest path to successful investing is to concentrate on the process of good investing, and let the results take care of themselves.

If you've made it to this point, I hope you thought it worth the time you invested in reading this book. So many investors spend so little time learning about investments, and then are frustrated when their investments disappoint them. I would never dream of walking into an operating room and performing surgery, but the average doctor thinks it should be easy to pick up the phone during a break and, with little or no training, compete with me in the world of investments.

A lot of studies point to the health benefits of regular exercise. Understanding more about how your body functions helps you maintain a healthy diet and improves the quality of your life. Perhaps you should look at improving your financial health as well by doing some regular financial exercises. If you could spend just one hour a week learning more about investments, reading a financial publication or book, or attending an investment seminar, you would increase your knowledge of investments and potentially improve your financial health. (By reading this book you get credit for two to four weeks of financial exercise. That wasn't bad, was it?)

I'm not saying you have to enjoy it. There are some nights that I don't feel like exercising, but I do it anyway, because I know it improves my body's ability to function well. We all have our own jobs, and usually receive money for the services we provide. We then have to do something with the money we earn. So many people are lost at this point. Knowing a little more about what to do with money will make life easier and allow you to function with less strain. It matters not what you have as your interests, your net worth, or your views of money. The more you know about managing money, the less frustration you will have with managing the money, and the greater likelihood you'll enjoy better performance.

If you decide to start learning more about investing, there's something I should tell you. No matter how hard you try, you will never know it all. I have been investing since I was 12 years old. It all started when I was delivering newspapers and investing the money I made in mutual funds. Almost 30 years later, I am still improving my skills. I know that I will never be a perfect investor, but I can enjoy the process of getting better at it. To me, it's a way of exercising my brain. Use it or lose it, as they say.

Challenge yourself to learn more about investing. You can certainly learn more than you know presently. *You can make a commitment to a lifelong process of becoming a better investor.* I know that the road to more knowledge will have its ups and downs, but I also know the trip will be very interesting and worthwhile.

I hope I've given you some food for thought, and that at this point you don't have knowledge indigestion. Finally, I wish you the best of success with your future investments.

Panic-Proof Investor Questions/Checklist _____

This is a summary of some of the practical points mentioned in this book. This checklist can be used to quickly refresh the investor on some of the important concepts in successfully investing one's assets. It might be used each time a new investment is considered simply to make sure you've considered the investment from a variety of viewpoints. For those who like to cheat and read the back of the book first, I encourage you to start at the beginning. There are a lot of subtle and useful thoughts and stories you'll miss out on by simply reading this checklist.

REQUIREMENTS FOR INVESTING SUCCESS

You must have an investment strategy that covers what and when you will buy or sell a category of investments.
You must have a money management strategy to control risk and diversify your portfolio.
You must understand yourself or you will not successfully accomplish the first two points on investment strategy and money management.

MONEY IS NOT EVIL

Money is simply money.
Separate self-worth from net worth.

YOUR BELIEFS BECOME YOUR WORLD

You perceive situations according to your beliefs.
Keep your mind flexible and open to new ideas.
If you have nonuseful beliefs, consider trying to change them.

BALANCE THE MENTAL SCENARIOS

What can go right?
What can go wrong?
What do I expect to happen?
Look at the investment with a balanced mind.

DEVELOP A PLAN TO GET OUT BEFORE GETTING IN

Where will you take a profit?
Where will you take a loss?
What are some of the things that might go wrong, and what will I do if they happen?

WRITE DOWN WHAT YOU EXPECT FROM THE INVESTMENT

Write down the best-case, worst-case, and expected-case scenario for the investment.

TRY TO MAKE MONEY FIRST, THEN PAY YOUR TAXES

Investing just to save taxes is a waste.
Tax laws are easily and frequently changed.

READ THE PAPERWORK

Be a good investment consumer.
You're paying for the legal disclosure anyway.
Take responsibility for your investments.

ALL RISKS ARE NOT CREATED EQUAL

Different investment returns usually come with different risks.
There are many forms of risk, not just risk of loss.

KEEP YOUR MONEY AWAY FROM THE PERSON MANAGING IT

Use a custodian to hold the assets and a manager or yourself to make the investment decisions.
Separating assets and manager provides cross-checks.

IF IT SOUNDS TOO GOOD TO BE TRUE, IT PROBABLY *IS* TOO GOOD TO BE TRUE

Don't be cynical and not check out a good deal.
However, be very cautious if it sounds too good.

TARGET A BALANCED STATE OF MIND

What are the positive and negative scenarios?
What are the expected scenarios?
This is the major difference between pros and rookies.

HAVE FUN OBSERVING THE MOVIE OF LIFE

Staying detached helps you stay balanced.
Target a detached state of mind when making major decisions.

GIVE YOURSELF ALTERNATE SCENARIOS

Stay flexible to new ideas.
Have a backup plan.
You can always dream up a negative scenario.

IF IT ISN'T BROKEN, DON'T FIX IT

Losing money is not a sufficient reason to stop an investment
program.
Look at the environment your investment has been in to help
decide how it has performed versus the benchmarks.

IT'S OKAY TO LOSE

Losing is a part of making money over the long run.

MAKE SURE THAT WHEN YOU LOSE, YOU HAVE ENOUGH LEFT TO CONTINUE TO PLAY THE GAME

Keep a portion of your assets liquid.
Invest only a portion of your assets in any single investment.

LET GAINS RUN; CUT LOSSES SHORT

One large gain can pay for many small losses.
Do not add to your losses.

PICK A REASONABLE TIME PERIOD FOR MONITORING

How much time can you allocate to monitoring? What is the shortest time frame that is meaningful in which you can take action?
What is the longest time frame that is meaningful over which you are letting the investment details get away from you?

OBSERVE THE ENVIRONMENT IN WHICH YOU ARE INVESTING

What is happening now in the world?
What changes might take place?
Use this information to be aware of the overall conditions your investment has faced.

HOW WILL YOUR INVESTMENT PERFORM IN VARIOUS ENVIRONMENTS?

Give yourself scenarios and benchmarks of how you would expect your investment to perform.
Be realistic, not optimistic or pessimistic.

EVERY INVESTMENT HAS RISK

If you think it doesn't, do some more homework.
Even T-Bills have certain risks.

NAVIGATE THE RIVER OF INVESTMENTS

When the flow of the market is in your direction, just steer the canoe to avoid trouble.
When the flow of the market is against you, paddle like crazy just to stay even.

AVOID CHASING THE HOT TRACK RECORD

That which is now hot, may soon be not.
Chasing the hot track record tends to keep you always one step behind the best investment.

CROWD PSYCHOLOGY IS USUALLY WRONG

It's better to be ahead of the crowd, not with them.
When everyone is talking about it, look out!
Some of the best opportunities are those investments deemed too dull, boring, or otherwise uninteresting to most investors.

A GOOD DEAL CAN GET EVEN BETTER

Investment sometimes can go to $0.
The current price is fair for buyer and seller or no trades will take place.

REPORTERS GIVE YOU WHAT THE PUBLIC WANTS TO READ

Ideas for articles come from the public's emotional needs and are usually slanted the wrong way at market exremes.
Read financial articles with a detached emotional attitude.

BEWARE OF THE EXTREMELY LONG TRACK RECORD

Are the same people managing it?
Will it continue?
A longer track record does not necessarily improve forecasting capability.

TOTAL RETURN IS NOT YIELD

Yield is interest or dividends received from an investment every month, quarter, or year.

Total return is yield plus any capital gains or minus any capital losses of the investment.

IMAGINE LIVING WITH THE INVESTMENT BEFORE BUYING IT

How fast does the investment move?

Will you be uncomfortable when it is down for a period?

IS THE TRACK RECORD REPRODUCIBLE?

Is there some reason the investment made money in the past?

Will that condition exist in the future?

MAKE A STRATEGIC DECISION TO GET INTO AND OUT OF AN INVESTMENT

Unless you are a professional trader, most decisions to buy or sell an investment should be made over longer-term time frames.

Make a strategic decision on getting out of an investment before you get into the investment.

STAY SLIGHTLY MORE CONSERVATIVE THAN YOU THINK YOU CAN TOLERATE

Pushing the limits just puts more pressure on you.

Investors are rarely dissatisfied with slower, smoother, more predictable performance.

DIVERSIFY TO YOUR COMFORT LEVEL

Spreading it around smoothes performance and helps you think strategically.

Diversifying by custodian or manager can help make your investments more safe.

DIVERSIFICATION CAN BE OVERDONE

Too many small pieces get to be a nuisance and lead to mediocrity.
Transaction costs are usually higher for small amounts of an investment than larger amounts of the same investment.
Try to achieve a balance between risk protection and transaction costs with your investments.

HOW IS EVERYONE COMPENSATED?

This gives a clue to everyone's possible motives.
Is a less expensive alternative available?
Is this appropriate for me or am I being sold the product because the brokerage firm is trying to market it?
How much of the broker/planner's total compensation is tied to selling this investment?
Can the fee or commission be negotiated?

AVOID INFORMATION OVERLOAD

Concentrate on facts, not opinions.
Form your own opinion.

COLLECT ENOUGH INFORMATION TO MAKE THE DECISION

You cannot collect facts forever.
Pick a reasonable time to gather facts.

MAKE A DECISION, THEN ACT!

Make most investment decisions strategically to avoid the pressure.

Concentrate on good investing discipline to make it easier to do the investment.

JUST PULL THE TRIGGER

When the sights are on the target, pull the trigger without second-guessing.

DOING NOTHING—THE TOUGHEST DECISION

If everything is performing as it was designed to do, then stay the course.
The big money is made just "sitting tight."

GOOD SERVICE DOESN'T EQUAL GOOD PERFORMANCE

Adequate service is important to help you feel comfortable with the investment.
Good service does not make up for poor investments.

TO SUCCEED, LOSE THE EGO

The markets are not to be feared or underestimated; they should be respected.
Self-confidence and ego are not the same.
Self-confidence is helpful to investors.
Egos get in the way of succeeding at almost anything.

YOUR PERSONAL LIFE AFFECTS YOUR SUCCESSES AND FAILURES

Take care of yourself as a person first.
This will help you be a better investor.

CONCENTRATE ON THE PROCESS OF GOOD INVESTING, AND LET THE RESULTS TAKE CARE OF THEMSELVES!

Focusing on things you can change helps put you in control of your life.

LOOK INTO THE INVESTING MIRROR

Investing is a mirror for your personality.
Have you matched the investment to yourself?

ENJOY THE PROCESS
OF GETTING BETTER AT INVESTING!
IT'S GOOD FOR YOUR FINANCIAL HEALTH.

Suggested Reading _____

For those who want to continue their education on how the mind can dramatically affect investing success, here are some publications that I found interesting.

Barach, Roland. *Mind Traps*. Dow-Jones-Irwin, 1988.

Douglas, Mark. *The Disciplined Trader*. Simon & Schuster, 1990.

Elder, Alexander. *Trading for a Living*. John Wiley and Sons, Inc., 1993.

Koppel, Robert, and Howard Abell. *The Innergame of Trading*. Probus Publishing Company, 1994.

Lefevre, Edwin. *Reminiscences of a Stock Market Operator*. George H. Doran Company, 1923.

Mackay, Charles. *Extraordinary Popular Delusions and the Madness of Crowds*. The Noonday Press, 1932.

Mamis, Justin. *The Nature of Risk*. Addison-Wesley Publishing Company, Inc., 1991.

Rosenberg, Claude, Jr., *Psycho-Cybernetics and the Stock Market*. Playboy Press, 1971.

Schwager, Jack. *Market Wizards*. Simon & Schuster, 1989.

Schwager, Jack. *The New Market Wizards*. HarperCollins, 1992.

Sloman, Jim, *Nothing*. *See* Tharp.

Tharp, Van K. *The Investment Psychology Guides*. Van Tharp Associates, 1985–91. (Available from Van Tharp Associates, 337 Lochside Drive, Cay, NC 27511; [919] 233-8855)